76.5

POETS' CORNER

POETS' CORNER

*

An anthology chosen and edited by

ELIZABETH
LONGFORD

Chapmans Publishers Limited
141–143 Drury Lane
London WC2B 5TB

BRITISH LIBRARY CATALOGUING IN PUBLICATION DATA
Poets' corner.
I. Longford, Elizabeth, *1906*–
821.91408

ISBN 1–85592–058–1

First published by Chapmans 1992

Designed by Ronald Clark

Photoset in Linotron Janson by
Rowland Phototypesetting Limited, Bury St Edmunds, Suffolk
Printed and bound in Great Britain by
Butler and Tanner Limited, Frome and London

Acknowledgments

I want to thank most warmly The Very Reverend
the Dean of Westminster, Michael Mayne,
and my publishers, Ian and Marjory Chapman,
who were jointly responsible for the idea of this anthology,
and whose help was as generous as it was essential.
I am most grateful to
the librarian of Westminster Abbey Library,
Mrs E. D. Nixon, and to the assistant librarian
for their valuable replies to my queries.
I also want to thank my editor, Yvonne Holland,
for her immensely perceptive and enthusiastic work;
Douglas Matthews, for the index;
my agent, Michael Shaw, for being as usual so encouraging;
Mr Alan Martin; my friend Marigold Johnson
for so kindly reading the text;
my friend Sir Nicholas Henderson for important information;
my daughters Antonia and Judith, my daughter-in-law Clare
and my husband, Frank.

Permissions Acknowledgments

The editor and publishers gratefully acknowledge permission to reproduce copyright material.

Richard Aldington: from *Collected Poems 1915–1923*, © the Estate of Richard Aldington. Reprinted by permission of Rosica Colin Limited.

W. H. Auden: 'Spain – April 1937' from *The English Auden*, edited by E. Mendelson. Reprinted by permission of Faber and Faber Ltd. 'At the Grave of Henry James' from *W. H. Auden: Collected Poems*, edited by E. Mendelson. Reprinted by permission of Faber and Faber Ltd. 'The Sea and the Mirror' from *For the Time Being*, copyright 1945 by W. H. Auden. Reprinted by permission of Faber and Faber Ltd.

Laurence Binyon: from *The Collected Poems of Laurence Binyon*. Reprinted by permission of Mrs Nicolete Gray and The Society of Authors on behalf of the Laurence Binyon Estate.

Edmund Blunden: from *The Collected Poems of Edmund Blunden*. Reprinted by permission of Peters, Fraser & Dunlop Ltd.

Nevill Coghill: from *The Canterbury Tales* by Geoffrey Chaucer, translated by Nevill Coghill (Penguin Classics, revised edition, 1977), copyright © 1951 by Nevill Coghill, 1958, 1960, 1975, 1977. Reprinted by permission of Penguin Books Ltd.

Noël Coward: 'Mad Dogs and Englishmen' from *Words and Music*, copyright © 1931 the Estate of Noël Coward. 'Dance Little Lady' from *This Year of Grace*, copyright © 1928 the Estate of Noël Coward. 'Poor Little Rich Girl' from *Charlot's Revue of 1926*, copyright © 1926 the Estate of Noël Coward. 'The Stately Homes of England' from *Operette*, copyright © 1938 the Estate of Noël Coward. Reprinted by permission of Michael Imison Playwrights Ltd, 28 Almeida Street, London N1 1TD.

T. S. Eliot: from *Collected Poems 1909–1962*. Reprinted by permission of Faber and Faber Ltd.

Contents

*

INTRODUCTION
page 1

*

POETS' CORNER
page 35

*

THE FIRST WORLD WAR POETS
page 191

*

POETS ELSEWHERE
IN THE ABBEY
page 229

*

INDEX
page 253

INTRODUCTION

Poets' Corner, in the south transept of Westminster Abbey, is crowded with tombs, statues, busts, plaques, tablets and floorstones. They are dedicated mainly to the memory of poets and writers; but also to a lesser number of artists, divines and politicians. This anthology is concerned only with the literary works of the poets and writers, and with their lives.

There is something fascinating about any corner. For most people since their childhood the corner has been a special place: secret and delightful but also vaguely threatening. Little Jack Horner (of the nursery rhyme) sat in the corner to eat his Christmas pie, and it was while he was there that he discovered the plum in the pie and said, 'What a good boy am I!' But bad boys were punished by being made to stand in the corner. So you can equally make a corner of the plums of life or be cornered, trapped.

In that second sense, death has cornered all the poets and so many others in this great building. James Shirley (born 1596) wrote:

> The glories of our blood and state
> Are shadows, not substantial things;
> There is no armour against fate;
> Death lays his icy hand on kings: . . .
> Only the actions of the just
> Smell sweet and blossom in their dust.

Sadly, many of the poets and writers whose works 'blossom' here were cornered long before their time. Such was the brevity of life in all but the modern era that the average age in Poets' Corner is no more than fifty to sixty years. Sadly, also, some of them died in extreme poverty, never guessing the glory that was to be theirs. William Mason, for instance, an eighteenth-century poet buried here, produced a terrifying list of the perils attendant on a scholar's life: toil, envy, hardship, inadequate patrons, stingy pensions, debts, prison. There were unfortunates who died in asylums. But here we must change our commiseration to something more like celebration. How amazing that John Clare and others should have written as they did in such surroundings. The poet's imagination can unlock the most formidable of gates.

In any case, the idea of mad poets seemed perfectly natural in the old days. Shakespeare linked the poet with the lunatic and the lover. Byron was said to be 'mad, bad, and dangerous to know'. Macaulay, in his essay on Milton, went further and suggested: 'Perhaps no person can be a poet, or can even enjoy poetry, without a certain unsoundness of mind . . .'

It is entirely appropriate that Westminster Abbey, a 'temple of English history' (Dean Michael Mayne), the 'national Valhalla' (A. N. Wilson), should have its corners. There is Innocents' Corner in the north aisle of Henry VII's chapel, where James I's two baby daughters are buried and perhaps also the bones of the Princes in the Tower. There is Whigs' Corner, as Dean Stanley used to call the area in which statesmen, including Charles James Fox, are commemorated and sometimes buried. But Poets' Corner is by far the largest, the most famous, the most enthralling of them all.

This introduction to my anthology of Poets' Corner will examine, first, how the poets and writers got there; secondly, the kind of options open to their anthologist. I must say at the outset what a unique experience it has been.

So much of English literature lay at peace before me, 'asleep in the Lord', as many Abbey tombs declare. Some of the poems I have chosen had become familiar literally at my mother's knee.

Gerard Manley Hopkins, seemed suddenly to come to life again as his memorial was unveiled at the Abbey service. (I sat in a pew with John Betjeman.)

One sees what an incomparably rich and complex thing this English poetic tradition is. There are so many 'fathers' of this or that: of verse first written in English, of blank verse, rhymed couplets, modern verse and verse without rhyme or metre. How essential to our continued national life are the inhabitants of Poets' Corner. Essential also in so many cases to the imaginative life of the whole world.

There are all those groups or schools of poets, some known by their period (Elizabethan poets, Restoration dramatists, Georgian poets); others by the descriptive titles that the critics have wished upon them (Metaphysicals, Classicists, Romantics). The glory of the Corner is as varied as the literature it represents, and I shall now look at some typical ways in which a writer might seem worthy of pulling out this plum.

Holders of the laureateship were obvious candidates. Indeed there are not a few poets laureate interred here. Ben Jonson, the first poet laureate of all, immediately comes to mind. Though buried elsewhere in the Abbey, he has his memorial in Poets' Corner. This having been said, the apparent rule must immediately be qualified – not an unusual situation here. Thomas Gray refused the laureateship; his memorial is nonetheless present. Again, Sir Walter Scott could have counted the laureateship among his many honours, but he chose not to do so. He too has his bust in Poets' Corner. At the other end of the scale appears Robert Bridges, Order of Merit and poet laureate. Inexplicably he is not here.

The failure of the laureateship to confer a certain claim on Poets' Corner, together with its absence being no deterrent, illustrates the capriciousness of choice. In that sense the Corner is characteristically British. There are no general rules of entry that cannot seemingly be broken. There is no abstract tidiness. The Corner has grown up organically without a written constitution, like the nation it represents.

The nation? Poets' Corner does not even confine itself entirely to one nation, to writers of British nationality. Henry James and T. S. Eliot were both born American citizens. But were they not naturalised British subjects? That is so. However, Henry Wadsworth Longfellow was an American citizen who did not become a British subject, yet is nevertheless memorialised in Poets' Corner. That might suggest that the only absolutely necessary qualification, on this level, was to write in the English language. Not so. Though Isaac Casaubon, a Swiss citizen naturalised English, neither wrote nor fully understood the English language, yet he made the grade. His works were translated from the Latin.

If anything is proved by these facts, it is simply that Poets'

Corner is as full of anomalies as all other favourite British institutions.

Casaubon brings me to an honourable and perhaps neglected group, the translators. John Keats adventured into the Homeric 'realms of gold' through the work of an early translator, Chapman. The experience left him stunned, like the explorers when they first sighted the Pacific and stood 'Silent upon a peak in Darien'. Fortunately Keats soon broke his silence with one of his most evocative sonnets: 'On First Looking into Chapman's Homer'. Before I could read any Greek plays in the original (with a crib), I revelled in Professor Gilbert Murray's translations of Euripides. Translators as a whole, however, have not fared particularly well at the hands of critics. Sir John Denham, one of the many seventeenth-century writers to be found in Poets' Corner, decided that a good translator was the exception not the rule. He wrote:

> Such is our pride, our folly, or our fate
> That few but such as cannot write, translate.

On the other hand, one can quote against Denham the quatrain by William Cowper, who is commemorated in the Abbey though not in Poets' Corner:

> It is a maxim of much weight,
> Worth conning o'er and o'er,
> He who has Homer to translate,
> Had need do nothing more.

This is not the place to discuss whether translators can ever be creators in the fullest sense. Instead I quote a brief episode from the life of Gilbert Murray, in which the point is neatly put. When one of his translations of a Euripides play was produced and received with rapturous applause and cries of 'Author!', the professor wittily took the curtain call with the words, 'The author is dead.' Even so it was the author Murray and not the author Euripides who got into Poets' Corner. Contrariwise, the poet Geoffrey Chaucer is in Poets' Corner, while Professor Nevill Coghill, despite his having made Chaucer available to so many readers through his Penguin verse translations, must merely be content with their gratitude.

Turning from the sublime Chaucer to some of the relatively unknown or even ridiculous writers who have entered Poets' Corner, how did these latter achieve such prominence? The answer is often simple. Either through their own money-bags or through the old boys' network of friends, relatives, pupils. In times past it was by no means impossible to leave money for a monument and for Dean and Chapter to oblige. Like the Order of the Garter in Lord Melbourne's day and in his words: there was 'no damned merit about it'.

Many of the distinguished writers and statesmen, however, who helped carry a coffin to a grave in Poets' Corner, clearly believed in their friend's genuine worth. Today it is hard to swallow the fact that the funeral of Isaac Casaubon, for example, was one of the most splendid recorded. Six bishops, two deans and almost the whole clergy of the metropolis were said to have followed the body to Westminster Abbey; the sermon was preached by his friend Bishop Overall of Lichfield; his monument paid for by his friend Thomas Morton, later Bishop of Durham. But we must not regard it as an ecclesiastical 'job'. The truth is that a famous divine such as Casaubon cut as much ice in the sixteenth and early seventeenth centuries as a leading actor does today.

A much better known but still not 'leading' poet, Abraham Cowley, also made a splash – his last splash – at his funeral. He had died somewhat ignominiously, according to John Aubrey, of a fever brought on by lying out in the fields after a drinking bout. No less a grandee than the Duke of Buckingham nevertheless held a tassel of the pall covering Cowley's coffin. He was buried next to Chaucer.

The 'old friends' network operated more attractively for the poet Thomas Gray and the playwright John Gay than it did for many others. Thomas Gray's fellow poet and admirer William Mason joined with two other admirers to erect a monument to their friend in Poets' Corner. It is immediately beneath that of Milton. John Gay also was buried here because he had affectionate and powerful friends; and he had affectionate and powerful friends because he was clever, good-tempered and amusing. His monument in Poets' Corner was paid for by his patrons the Duke and Duchess of Queensberry. Beside these, the Earl of Chesterfield and Viscount Cornbury, Gay's funeral was attended by General Dormer and Alexander Pope, not to mention a bishop to conduct the choral service, with a full choir. How poignant that *The Beggar's Opera* should have earned Gay a musical send-off. For once the juxtaposition of tombs in Poets' Corner seemed exactly right, Gay's and Chaucer's being near neighbours.[1] Chaucer's Wife of Bath from *The Canterbury Tales* and Gay's Polly from *The Beggar's Opera* would have understood one another very well. *Polly*, the sequel to *The Beggar's Opera*, was publicised in Gay's lifetime by being banned by Sir Robert Walpole, England's first prime minister, for satirising him and his political party. 'The inoffensive John Gay', wrote Dr Arbuthnot to his friend Jonathan Swift, 'is now become one of the obstructions to the peace of Europe, the terror of the Ministers . . .' Only a few more years were to pass before Walpole as well as Gay would be laid to rest in the same Abbey among the great and the good.

It is not always easy to decide why certain poets who seemed likely candidates for Poets' Corner in fact never made it. Dr Johnson gives his own explanation for one such failure. His interesting theory may throw light on some general principles. George, 1st Baron Lyttelton, another eighteenth-century poet, failed because he did not work hard enough at his verses. Though a precocious scholar of Eton College, he later allowed politics to compete with poetry. If he had given more time to poetry, wrote Dr Johnson, 'he might have achieved literary excellence'. As it was, his real contribution to literature was generous patronage of poets less well endowed than himself. Of Lyttelton's own poems Johnson wrote: 'They have nothing to be despised and little to be admired'; of his epigrams and songs: they were 'sometimes sprightly and sometimes insipid'. From Johnson's account of Lyttelton one can see clearly how right were the many poets buried in Poets' Corner to give up other professions – often

[1] Gay's memorial is no longer in Poets' Corner but in the triforium. It was moved there during preparation of the wooden galleries that were erected in the transept at the time of the 1937 Coronation, when the thirteenth-century wall paintings were found on the wall behind where Gay's memorial stood. It has never reappeared.

the law – for full-time writing. Literature is a demanding mistress.

Curiously enough, Dr Johnson seems almost to contradict himself when he begins to censure a major poet – no Lyttelton, this – for concentrating on his poetry rather than his life. Thomas Gray, famous author of what has come to be called familiarly 'Gray's Elegy', struck Johnson as being a more admirable man than poet. The learned author of *Lives of the Poets* particularly applauded Gray because he 'had the honour of refusing the laurel'; though he may have implied that Gray did not deserve the laureateship anyway. Johnson was at his most tetchy, yet amusing, in criticising Gray's other most famous poem, 'Prospect of Eton'. In the poem, Gray, himself an Old Etonian, uses poetic licence to ask the River Thames, on which Eton is situated, what the boys of the college are doing these days. Sarcastically Dr Johnson comments that Gray's 'supplication' of Father Thames 'to tell him who drives the hoop or tosses the ball is useless and puerile. Father Thames has no better means of knowing than Gray himself.' Fortunately this pleasant pedantry was not successful in keeping Gray out of Poets' Corner.

William Davenant, a seventeenth-century dramatist, is another type of exception to Dr Johnson's rule. His life as a Cavalier poet was highly coloured. He had ammunition illegally supplied to the royalist cause, earning the title of 'the great pirate', and though Pepys admired his satirical drama, *The Wits*, Davenant was more of a 'character' than an artist. Yet he followed Ben Jonson as England's second poet laureate and so had no difficulty in achieving fame in Poets' Corner. John Aubrey suggested that Davenant fell short of total success when his coffin entered the Abbey unadorned by a laurel wreath. On the other hand, Aubrey found an adequate laurel decorating his engraved portrait in the Bodleian Library at Oxford. Today, alas, both pirate and poet are forgotten. Davenant's works stand forlornly in what Macaulay called 'the dust and silence of the upper shelf'.

To me, the selection of poets for the Corner is seen at its oddest in the case of Francis Beaumont and John Fletcher. The Elizabethan-Jacobean partnership was one of the closest in English literature. The two friends were said by Aubrey to have shared a house, a bed, a wench, clothes, a cloak – and of course a pen. But when it came to the literary day of judgment, one was taken and the other left. Francis Beaumont got into Poets' Corner, John Fletcher did not. Yet Fletcher was by no means the inferior poet of the two. His beautiful *Faithful Shepherdess* (probably all his own work) is steeped in melodious imagery; he may even have had a hand in Shakespeare's *Henry VIII*. Then why the break-up in the partnership with Beaumont?

When I began my work on this anthology I found that Beaumont's and – as I thought – Fletcher's memorial floor-stone was literally under the counter. An immensely heavy counter covered several of the engraved slabs on the floor of Poets' Corner. The combined efforts of the staff and myself failed to roll away the counter from the stone; but the splendid Westminster Abbey guide to Poets' Corner informs us that *two* Beaumonts (one of them a minimal poet) rather than one Beaumont and one Fletcher are commemorated beneath. It was not that Fletcher came of an inferior family. Born in Rye, Sussex, Fletcher was the son of a clergyman. Some might think that this alone should have been a key to the Corner, judging by the number of clergymen's sons to win places. Fletcher's family were also noted for their literary interests, especially his Uncle Giles, Cousin Giles and Cousin Phineas. True, his father helped to see Mary, Queen of Scots into the next world – he was officially present at her execution; but he himself died of the plague, which was surely expiation enough. Then what was it that kept John Fletcher out? Can it be that the authorities felt the famous partnership had gone too far and that in death they should be divided? Probably we shall never know.

It would perhaps be easier to understand the sometimes erratic choices of writers for Poets' Corner if we had a detailed picture of popular taste at any given period and, more important, of its incessant changes. Dr Johnson, as ever, stands out as a pungent guide to his period. We may not agree with him, but he does show us what was expected of poets in the seventeenth and eighteenth centuries – or rather, what *he*, the incomparable pundit, expected of them. His strictures on John Philips' use of blank verse, for instance, make one wonder how Philips ever succeeded in scaling the high walls of Johnson's ridicule to reach Poets' Corner on the other side. Johnson's law was Miltonic: every would-be poet should do as Milton did, that is, use blank verse for subjects of solemn import *(Paradise Lost)*, but rhyme for lighter subjects. Thus poor Philips' choice of blank verse for a poem on *cider*, of all things, was absolutely misjudged. 'Contending angels may shake the regions of heaven in blank verse,' wrote the outraged Doctor, but 'the embellishment of rhyme must recommend to our attention the art of grafting, and decide the merits of the *redstreak* [cider apple] and *pearmain*.' Other critics, however, found *Cyder* and Philips so much to their taste that they made absurd comparisons (as we would think today) between Philips and his contemporaries. One admirer wrote:

> Oh various bard! you all our powers control,
> You now disturb and now divert the soul;
> Milton and Butler in thy muse combine;
> Above the last thy many beauties shine.

Dr Johnson at any rate would have agreed with this dig at Samuel Butler, author of the fantastically popular narrative poem, *Hudibras*, and in Poets' Corner along with Johnson himself, Milton and Philips. In this overrated work, Dr Johnson decided that 'there is more said than done. It is indeed much more easy to form dialogues than to contrive adventures.' The Doctor demanded many more interruptions in the dialogue, adding, 'The great source of pleasure is in variety.' He would have been staggered by the fulsome praise heaped upon the second-rate Philips for his poem on *Blenheim* by another friend, the poet Thomas Tickell (not in the Corner):

> Unfetter'd in great Milton's strain he writes,
> Like Milton's angels while his hero fights;
> Pursues the bard[1] where he with honour can,
> Equals the poet and excels the man.

After this extraordinary effusion it is worth looking at Poets' Corner today. Every visitor will have heard of Milton, a few of

[1] Milton.

Samuel Butler (though they may confuse him with his nineteenth-century namesake, author of *The Way of All Flesh*, who is not in Poets' Corner), probably none of John Philips.

A straightforward case of change (and improvement) in public taste is illustrated by two dramatists: one forgotten, the other famous, both thoroughly allergic to each other while alive. Richard Cumberland (born 1732) pandered successfully to the bourgeois taste for 'tame and tearful synthetic comedy', writes M. Billington. Along came Richard Sheridan (born 1751) whose astringent satire of high society drove Cumberland's feeble efforts off the stage. I would hazard a guess that if Cumberland had been born *after* instead of before Sheridan, i.e. by the time public taste had changed, he would never have found a place in Poets' Corner. The change of course was brought about quite simply by the arrival of a genuine talent.

Not that the good Doctor confined his criticism to the weaker brethren featuring in his *Lives of the Poets*. The great Joseph Addison himself, an essayist of unassailable renown, could not venture into the realms of poetry without risking a sharp attack. One of Addison's rhymed couplets particularly aroused Johnson's scorn. Addison had written:

> I bridle in my struggling Muse with pain,
> That longs to launch into a nobler strain.

Johnson pounced on these harmless but mixed metaphors about the muse with avidity:

> To *bridle* a *goddess* is no very delicate idea; but why must she be *bridled*? because she *longs to launch*; an act which was never hindered by a *bridle*: and whither will she *launch*? into a *nobler strain*. She is in the first line a *horse*, in the second a *boat*; and the care of the poet is to keep his *horse* or his *boat* from singing.

Maybe this clever but ridiculous nit-picking would have made Addison laugh, if not turn in his grave.

No doubt some of Johnson's entertaining acerbity as a critic was due to the constant bickering among the eighteenth-century writers and poets. Alexander Pope, a close associate of both Joseph Addison and the minor poet Nicholas Rowe, decided to heal a coolness that had developed between his two friends.[1] So when a piece of good fortune befell Addison, Pope told him how unfeignedly pleased Rowe was. To which Addison replied: 'I do not suspect that he feigned; but the levity of his heart is such, that he is struck with any adventure; and it would affect him just in the same manner if he heard I was going to be hanged.' Dr Johnson's final comment on this dialogue between Pope and Addison – for it was Johnson who collected this piece of gossip – was typically dismissive: 'Perhaps the best advice to authors', he wrote, 'would be that they should keep out of the way of one another.'

Yet here they all, or at least many of them, are, gathered together in Poets' Corner. In life they may have been at loggerheads but in death they were not divided.

It seems that poets and writers were somewhat less abusive of each other in the century that followed. However, two of the famous nineteenth-century names commemorated here kept the flag of invective flying in their time. Robert Southey was lambasted by Lord Byron, who called the poet laureate 'turncoat Southey' or, for good measure, 'shuffling Southey, that incarnate lie'. At the other end of the century the much respected John Ruskin launched a vicious attack upon James McNeill Whistler's painting called *Nocturne in Black and Gold*:

I have seen and heard much of Cockney impudence before now; but never expected to hear a coxcomb ask two hundred guineas for flinging a pot of paint in the public's face.

Ruskin is safe in Poets' Corner, free from Cockney painters or American coxcombs. But neither William Makepeace Thackeray nor George Eliot, two of the most distinguished novelists in Poets' Corner, escaped being savaged by the redoubtable Ruskin. 'Thackeray', he wrote, 'settled like a meat-fly on whatever one

---

[1] Addison is in Poets' Corner, Rowe in the triforium and as for Pope, I hope his name will one day join theirs. See page 25.

had for dinner, and made one sick of it.' While George Eliot's work he compared to 'the sweepings of a Pentonville omnibus', Pentonville being the road in London where was situated the notorious prison.

Exaggerated praise of one poet by another is the opposite side of the coin. We have already heard of the poet Tickell comparing Philips to Milton – to the latter's distinct disadvantage. And Shakespeare himself was subjected to odious comparisons. On the tomb of Nicholas Rowe – he whom Addison so much disliked and despised – these improbable words appear.

> Thy Reliques *Rowe*! to this sad shrine we trust,
> And near thy *Shakespeare* place thy honour'd Bust:
> Oh next him skill'd to draw the tender tear,
> For never Heart felt Passion more sincere.

So now we know who was Shakespeare's runner-up.

Abraham Cowley, as we have seen, was another poet who received undeserved adulation. His contemporary biographer, Dr Sprat, considered Cowley's two greatest predecessors to be Chaucer and Spenser – no mention of Shakespeare who was presumably left to fight it out with Cowley for third place. King Charles II went even further, declaring after Cowley's death in 1667: 'Mr Cowley has not left a better man behind him in England.' Best of all, Cumberland (already mentioned) had a friend Dr Drake who said Cumberland 'happily combined the excellencies of Shakespeare and Milton'.

Several of the most illustrious names to be found in Poets' Corner were latecomers. William Shakespeare himself stands out among them. Dying in 1616, he was buried in his home town, Stratford-upon-Avon. It was not till 1740 that a statue was erected in Poets' Corner to his memory. Meanwhile poets, writers and dramatists had made their way, in ever increasing numbers, into the poets' Valhalla. Perhaps some literary dean or canon, saying his prayers one day in the south transept – the actual position of Poets' Corner – caught the eye of Chaucer and suddenly asked himself:

'Why no Shakespeare?' The truth was that there had been a move to bury, or rather, re-bury Shakespeare in Poets' Corner soon after his death. But the move was rightly opposed, particularly by Shakespeare's admirer and fellow poet, Ben Jonson, who wrote:

> My Shakespeare, rise! I will not lodge thee by
> Chaucer or Spenser or bid Beaumont lie
> A little further on to make thee room.

The monument to Shakespeare was finally raised by public subscription, Pope being one of those involved, as well as the actor Garrick. (Garrick himself is here; Pope surprisingly not.)

Chaucer and Spenser were the first two poets to be buried in the east aisle of the south transept. It was Ben Jonson who had first called Shakespeare 'Sweet Swan of Avon', and Ben had no wish for Will to become a swan of the Thames.

When a monument to Shakespeare was finally decided upon, one hundred and twenty-four years after his death, it did him proud. Designed by William Kent, it was executed by Peter Scheemakers, who was responsible also for the bust of John Dryden in Poets' Corner and many other sculptures in the Abbey. The expression on Shakespeare's face is somewhat secretive, as if he realised that they had used the wrong version of Prospero's great speech ('Our revels now are ended') on the scroll he is holding.

Another latecomer was John Milton. Political prejudice against such an outright Parliamentarian as Milton kept out for sixty-three years the man whose name would, as the royalists believed, have polluted the Abbey's walls. The fine bust by John Michael Rysbrack shows Milton looking suitably sad and noble.

It is not difficult to find reasons beside politics why some poets got in at once, while others arrived only after an interval, long or short. Edmund Spenser, the Elizabethan 'Prince of Poets', was buried by general poetical consent in what was later to become Poets' Corner. It was said that all the poets were present. They all, Shakespeare probably among them, had ready the pens and paper on which they had written their elegies to Spenser. They threw them into Spenser's grave. What was thought to be

Spenser's grave was opened in November 1938. No elegies were found.

The lateness of some nineteenth-century arrivals can be put down to moral objections. Shelley was a revolutionary atheist; Byron was 'dangerous to know' according to Lady Caroline Lamb, his mistress and wife of Lord Melbourne, Queen Victoria's first prime minister. I cannot imagine many good nineteenth-century prebends or sub-deans lamenting the absence of Byron or Shelley. Indeed, if it had not been for the labours of the Keats-Shelley Memorial Association and the Poetry Society, I doubt if they would have entered Poets' Corner when they did: Shelley in 1954, Byron in 1969.[1]

Another category of late or non-arrivals is women. This is hardly surprising, since women have been late arrivals everywhere. Jane Austen received a small tablet (one might say tiny, compared with some of the colossal monuments), beautifully engraved, in 1967. She would probably have thought it entirely suitable. Again, without the urgency of a literary society – the Jane Austen Society – she might not be there. A plaque to the three Brontë sisters had already arrived twenty years earlier. (We look for a Brontë Society and find one.) Lastly there is George Eliot (Mary Ann Evans, later Mrs Cross), by many considered the greatest novelist of her age. Five women to eighty-five men. Seventeen to one. And the point is rubbed in by four of the five women having published under men's names. Perhaps we can draw some slight comfort from the fact that in the Abbey's east walk there is another woman writer, Aphra Behn, the seventeenth-century novelist and dramatist. Keeping her company are two famous actresses, Anne Bracegirdle and Mrs Betterton, as well as the wife and daughter of a royal chaplain and the daughter of an eighteenth-century politician. Even the ratio of women to men is here rather better: six to twenty – though only three of the six women are there in their own right.

Visitors to Poets' Corner are fond of asking two apparently simple questions. Who was the first poet, writer or dramatist to be commemorated here? Who was the last?

[1] Lord Abinger, a member of the Keats-Shelley Association, was to become vice-president of the future Byron Society, re-founded in 1971.

Like many simple historical questions, the answers are complex. To begin with, what exactly is meant by the 'first' poet? If it means the first chronologically, the monk Caedmon has that honour. However, his remains must have been laid to rest in his monastery church some time towards the end of the seventh century. He is honoured here in Poets' Corner by a stone in the floor that is far from being the first stone to be placed there.

So who is the first actually to be buried in Poets' Corner? Chaucer, of course, though not without a curious internal migration. He died in 1400 and his grave was in the Abbey floor (under the present bookstall). One hundred and fifty-six years passed. Then, in 1556, his remains were transferred to a sculptured tomb erected in his memory by a minor poet named Nicholas Brigham. Alas poor Brigham. This was his only personal entry into Poets' Corner and even the traces of this distinction have almost vanished. According to the absorbing *Official Guide* to Westminster Abbey and Poets' Corner by a series of authorities culminating in E. D. Nixon (1988), Brigham's memorial portrait of Chaucer included a second figure thought to be Brigham himself. Last visible in the eighteenth century, this second figure is now obliterated, though his name is still visible on Chaucer's tomb.

Forty-three years after Chaucer's re-burial in Poets' Corner he was joined by Edmund Spenser, who died in 1599.

Who, then, was the last? If this second question is to be treated on a par with the first, it means 'Who was the last poet, writer or dramatist to be *buried* in Poets' Corner?' As one would imagine, growing congestion has resulted in fewer and fewer writers being actually buried here. In any case, those buried here have always, since the sixteenth century, been outnumbered by those with monuments only – ranging from plain memorial stones to elaborate statuary. The actual burials of most of our poets have taken place all over the country and indeed all over the world: Austria (Auden), Dublin (Hopkins), Rome (Keats and Shelley), the United States (Longfellow and Henry James), Scotland (Burns and Scott), Wales (Dylan Thomas), Australia (Adam Lindsay Gordon). Incidentally, this last-mentioned poet, A. L. Gordon, whose bust was unveiled in 1934 by the then Duke of York (later

King George VI) to mark Gordon's centenary, is the only one whose bust looks like the popular idea of a young poet. Placed on the same column as Tennyson's but on the other side of it, Gordon's bust would do quite well for Rupert Brooke or even an updated Byron. The sculptor was Lady Kennet.

The last poet to be buried in Poets' Corner was John Masefield; his ashes were laid here in 1967. The ashes of Professor Gilbert Murray were buried here in 1957 and those of Thomas Hardy in 1928, though Hardy's heart was buried in Dorset.

As for the latest memorial (as distinct from burial) to a poet, this is at present (until Trollope arrives; see page 23) to John Clare unveiled in June 1989, preceded by Matthew Arnold in February 1989 and Edward Lear in June 1988. Of the poet Clare the Dean writes, 'I asked myself to put Clare in as nobody else, so far as I can see, had ever requested him!' A plaque to the working-class Nottinghamshire poet and novelist of original genius, D. H. Lawrence, was unveiled by the poet Ted Hughes, poet laureate, on 16 November 1985.

Five days earlier there had been a new, composite arrival: a large, magnificent stone was laid in the floor of Poets' Corner and unveiled by the same Ted Hughes on 11 November 1985. The date – the sixty-seventh Armistice Day after the Great War – should make everyone realise for whom the stone speaks. It is for the sixteen poets who fought – and many of them died – in 1914–1918. The longest lived of these First World War poets was Robert Graves. He died in 1985. The youngest was Edmund Blunden (born 1896). It was Blunden who said of them that they showed the English to be no longer a nation of shopkeepers but a nation of poets.

Yet if one examines the parentage of writers honoured in Poets' Corner, there are plenty of shopkeepers among them. Very few of them were of aristocratic birth; several were sons of inn-keepers or vintners. We do not know how many of their mothers served in shops or were barmaids. What we do know is that a remarkable proportion of our poets were brought up in a manse or rectory. In other words, they were the sons of clergy, presumably with mothers who were also literate. The winning clergyman is that obstreperous Irishman of considerable talent, the Revd Patrick

Brontë who, with his cultured Cornish wife, produced *three* poets. The winning combination of schools and universities was Westminster and Cambridge: five poets or writers having attended both. Perhaps this is to be expected in view of the close connection between the school and the Abbey: the one catering for the poet's beginning, the other for his end. I have mentioned as often as possible a poet's schooling, which ranges here from the elitism of Eton and Harrow, Winchester and Rugby, St Paul's and Westminster, to the village dame school, for which the poor parents had to save and scrape. On epitaphs, Macaulay noted a strange eighteenth-century preference for Latin, the pundits refusing to 'pollute' the walls of the Abbey with English epitaphs. You might as well argue, said Macaulay ironically, for Greek inscriptions on Roman triumphal arches or Egyptian hieroglyphics on Greek tombs. Macaulay can see no reason for celebrating 'a British writer in Latin'.

Four of the English epitaphs in Poets' Corner seem to me as beautiful and appropriate as possible: the Brontë sisters' 'With courage to endure', John Clare's 'Fields were the essence of the song', Byron's 'But there is that within me which shall tire / Torture and Time, and breathe when I expire' and Dylan Thomas's 'Time held me green and dying / Though I sang in my chains like the sea'.

Some of the memorials, old and new, give special character to Poets' Corner. I admire the dimpled Dryden with his slight smile, as if he had just won an argument with one of his quarrelsome contemporaries. Longfellow is a wonderful bearded prophet. Michael Drayton, nearby, is elegant and serious. I am enthralled by the vastness of the monument to Matthew Prior – very necessary, apparently, to accommodate the enormous list of his virtues. William Mason's Latin inscription I like very much (despite Macaulay) – 'Optimo viro, poetae, cultuo, casto, pio' – though his absolute chastity and piety are rendered less than obvious by a jolly self-indulgent double-chin. Thomas Campbell, a minor nineteenth-century poet, is engagingly represented in the same pose as neighbouring Shakespeare. James Thomson, author of 'Rule Britannia', looks beguilingly like a male Britannia, if only he had the requisite shield and trident. I pick out Oliver Goldsmith's interesting, ugly physiognomy, Burns' handsome face and Tennyson's expression, with its surprising touch of arrogance. Thackeray's face is the work of that Baron Marochetti who was responsible, among other major works, for the affectionate statues of Queen Victoria and Prince Albert in the Frogmore Mausoleum. An enormous Addison looks across the plaques dedicated to Dickens and Kipling at an equally imposing Campbell. A prebendary of the Abbey, the Revd Thomas Triplet, occupies a grave that faces that of Thomas Parr across the way. Thomas Triplet was buried in Poets' Corner as a divine, distinguished for his culture, piety and generosity – generosity probably being the operative word. Thomas Parr must be here because he lived to be 152 years old, seeing out the reigns of nine monarchs and dying under the tenth, Charles I, in 1635.

On a marble pillar, surrounded by the wooden seats of living worshippers, is perhaps the most outstanding bust of all. William Blake, visionary painter and poet of England's green and pleasant land, was sculpted by Jacob Epstein, his bronze bust having been unveiled in 1957, Blake's bicentenary. One could read into his expression a stern awareness that his countrymen, even after two hundred years, have not yet built Jerusalem. Poets' Corner is full of fine sculpture by famous artists like Rysbrack, Scheemakers, Roubillac, Nollekens and Westmacott. But to a twentieth-century eye, the combination of Blake and Epstein is unbeatable.

One further aspect of Poets' Corner may be dealt with here, before I explain, very briefly, how I have constructed my anthology. Today the prospect of further additions to Poets' Corner is much in the news. The two chief limitations on this agreeable prospect are time and space. The *time* a poet must have been dead before his or her case can be advanced is usually ten years. Moreover they must be reasonably certain of recognition in 100 years' time. It is an easy guess that Sir John Betjeman, poet laureate, will be here in due course, if only for his good-humoured warning to all church architects, sung to S. Wesley's tune written for S. J. Stone's 'The Church's One Foundation':

The Church's restoration
In eighteen eighty-three
Has left for contemplation
Not what there used to be . . .

I hope that another recent laureate, Cecil Day-Lewis, will also be here.

The problem becomes complicated and difficult when *space* is considered. A flood of absent names comes to mind whose introduction into Poets' Corner would be an ornament to the Abbey, but whose numbers might be a headache. The Dean is alone responsible for admissions, though he will always consult his colleagues on Chapter. They are rightly not going to be pushed around by any special pleading from societies or individuals. The arguments for caution over admissions are strong. They are borne out by some of the early poets and playwrights already installed. Who would suggest that a minor playwright like Sir Robert Stapylton (died 1669) would ever have got in if he had had to wait for 100 years? Yet that interval might not have proved long enough, since in 1812 he was still said by his admirers to be assured of a place in the world's 'temple of immortality'.

On the other hand, Poets' Corner is a *national* Valhalla, and there are many glittering names in the starry firmament of national literature for whom no one has made an effective push, but whose absence is clearly regrettable. In order to improve the showing of women writers I would certainly press for Christina Rossetti (1830–1894), who never married but wrote some of the most moving love lyrics in the language: 'A Birthday' ('My heart is like a singing bird') and 'Song' ('When I am dead, my dearest'). Two other women I would suggest are Virginia Woolf for her incalculable influence on English prose, and Edith Sitwell for her poetic thought and style: 'Love is not changed by death, / And nothing is lost, / And all in the end is harvest.'

I realise that a humanist like Virginia Woolf at first may not seem to fulfil another condition laid down by the Dean and Chapter; a condition that is distinctly more subtle than 'time and space'. When the extremely civilised and sensitive Michael Mayne became Dean, he said that he and his colleagues would ask, 'Was this person so militantly atheist that it would destroy his integrity to fetch him into the church?' This is a question of interpretation. I remember the poet William Plomer saying at the time of Lord Byron's admission in 1969, that the poet's ghost must have viewed proceedings with a cynical smile. An enjoyable thought. All the same, Byron was by no means a militant atheist. He sent his daughter Allegra to an Italian convent and was himself buried in Hucknall Torkard church, in ground that was, in its own way, no less sacred than Poets' Corner.

Of course there may be extreme cases that do not need inter-preting. The anti-monarchist writer, W. T. Stead, advocated turning Buckingham Palace into a Home for Fallen Women. He had every right to his view, but did not expect to be received at Queen Victoria's court. There may be an insane anti-Christian who wants Westminster Abbey to be transformed into the world's biggest Bingo Hall with Poets' Corner for the Ladies and Gents. He would not expect to be buried here even if he had written great poetry – which seems unlikely.

Returning to the possible. If Poets' Corner ever has a brother-and-sister duo (for Christina Rossetti might bring in her brilliant brother Dante Gabriel, Pre-Raphaelite poet and painter) it should also have a husband and wife: Elizabeth Barrett as well as Robert Browning. Typically, Robert's body was brought back from Italy, where he died in 1889, to be buried in Poets' Corner, while that of Elizabeth, his wife, who had died in Italy 28 years earlier, was left there. Nothing that Robert wrote is more gently and truly poetic than Elizabeth's affirmation of the divine peace:

Oh, the little birds sang east, and the little birds sang west –
Toll slowly
And I smiled to think God's greatness flowed around our
incompleteness –
Round our restlessness, His rest.

Elizabeth Barrett (1806–1861) was born in Durham, the daughter of a wealthy plantation owner. An invalid tyrannised over by her possessive father, she eloped with Browning in 1846, to enjoy a short, blissful marriage. It may have been her audacious attitude to women, expressed in *Aurora Leigh*, that kept her out of Poets' Corner, coupled with her advanced views on Italian liberation.

Politics – those of the English civil wars – may also have kept out two poets of genius. Edmund Waller and Andrew Marvell are both absent, I suspect because they both played ambivalent parts in the wars, Marvell being Oliver Cromwell's laureate. Yet we could not do without Waller's lyric 'Go, lovely Rose'. For his heroic couplets Dryden nominated Waller 'father of our English numbers'. Such was the wit and charm of his table-talk that he was said to be the only water-drinker welcome at banquets.

Two lines from Andrew Marvell's poem 'The Garden' have long been quoted and requoted because of their magical beauty: 'Annihilating all that's made / To a green thought in a green shade.' Six other lines from 'To His Coy Mistress' are equally well-known:

> But at my back I always hear
> Time's wingèd chariot hurrying near
> And yonder all before us lie
> Deserts of vast eternity. . . .
> The grave's a fine and private place,
> But none I think do there embrace.

Son of a Yorkshire clergyman, Marvell was MP for Hull and served under his great friend Milton in the office of Latin Secretary to the Council. Milton owed his release from prison to Marvell, and to Marvell the Dissenters owed many pungent airings of the arguments for freedom of worship. It was to take some 300 years for Marvell's greatness to be fully appreciated. He now deserves the seal of Poets' Corner.

Approaching nearer to our own day, there are two names that may have been controversial in the past but whose poetry and prose are now an essential part of our English heritage. Oscar Fingal O'Flahertie Wills Wilde (1854–1900) was brought up in Dublin, his father being a distinguished Irish doctor and his mother a clever writer who used the stylish pen name 'Speranza'. Wilde shone at Magdalen College, Oxford, married and had two sons, living in Tite Street, Chelsea. But he was an aesthete of the 'naughty nineties' breed. In 1890 he published *The Picture of Dorian Gray* in which an avowed homosexual, Lord Ronald Gower, was featured as Lord Henry Wotton. His brilliant play, *The Importance of Being Earnest*, was produced in the same year, 1895, as he was imprisoned in Reading Gaol for homosexual offences. He died a Catholic in Paris. In the present age, when penal reform has touched the nation's conscience, Wilde's *The Ballad of Reading Gaol* is unforgettable. (The Ballad was written 'In Memoriam C. T. W. Sometime Trooper of the Royal Horse Guards. Obiit H. M. Prison, Reading, Berkshire July 7, 1896'.)

> In Reading gaol by Reading town
>   There is a pit of shame
> And in it lies a wretched man
>   Eaten by teeth of flame,[1]
> In a burning winding-sheet he lies,
>   And his grave has got no name. . . .
>
> And there till Christ call forth the dead,
>   In silence let him lie:
> No need to waste the foolish tear,
>   Or heave the windy sigh:
> The man had killed the thing he loved,[2]
>   And so he had to die.
>
> And all men kill the thing they love,
>   By all let this be heard,
> Some do it with a bitter look,
>   Some with a flattering word,
> The coward does it with a kiss
>   The brave man with a sword!

And for those who prefer Wilde's scintillating witticisms, there is always his memorable dismissal of coffee: 'What is life without coffee?' – 'What is life *with* coffee?'

---

[1] Quick lime.   [2] His wife.

William Butler Yeats (1865–1939), son and brother of notable Irish painters, was born in Dublin but educated in London. Without even mentioning Yeats's early lyrics and plays, it is only necessary to quote his two famous lines on the Anglo-Irish 'Troubles' to realise that few modern political commentators will not have quoted them at least once, as an illustration of the modern world's psychological dilemma:

> The best lack all conviction, while the worst
> Are full of passionate intensity.

Meanwhile the Dean and Chapter have found a solution to the congestion of Poets' Corner. The notice, 'House Full' will be modified by the utilisation of window space. There is room for about thirty names to be inscribed on the plain glass of the great east window of the south transept, and plans are already in hand (1991) to invite artists to submit designs for it. Thirty sounds such a wonderfully generous number that I am tempted to add a few more names to my list. But first a word about Anthony Trollope who has been accepted by the Dean and is probably at the head of the list of those to be memorialised in the new window.

Anthony Trollope (1815–1882) was born in London and had a successful novelist for a mother and a failure for a father. His own first 'Barsetshire' novel, *The Warden*, appeared when he was forty, and his first 'political' novel, *Can You Forgive Her?*, three years before he retired as a distinguished civil servant at the Post Office in 1867. His popularity as a prolific Victorian novelist whose characters made serial appearances for the first time in England, was rightly revived in the twentieth century: by extensive reading during the black-out of the Second World War, and by television. The Abbey is full of monuments to dukes, hereditary and created. Trollope's fictional Duke of Omnium speaks better for them than most of them did for themselves. Trollope was fascinated by people, whether they were dukes or deans. As John Major, the Prime Minister and member of the Trollope Society, said at their celebration on 20 November 1991 of Trollope's acceptance for Poets' Corner: 'I admire his ability to create three-dimensional characters in their own world.'

In *Can You Forgive Her?* Mr Plantagenet Palliser, MP, the future Duke of Omnium (Planty Pal to his friends), has promised to take his wife, Lady Glencora, and her cousin Alice on a year's tour of the Continent. By the time they reach Paris, after a dreadful sea crossing, Palliser is regretting his decision.

'We can get to the Kurds, Alice, [says Lady Glencora] without getting into a packet again. That, to my way of thinking, is the great comfort of the Continent. One can go everywhere without being sea-sick.'

Mr Palliser said nothing, but he sighed as he thought of being absent for a whole year. He had said that such was his intention, and would not at once go back from what he himself had said. But how was he to live for twelve months out of the House of Commons? What was he to do with himself, with his intellect and his energy, during all these coming dreary days? And then – he might have been Chancellor of the Exchequer! He might even now, at this very moment have been upon his legs, making a financial statement of six hours' duration, to the delight of one-half of the House, and bewilderment of the other, instead of dragging cloaks across that dingy, dull, dirty waiting-room at the Paris Station, in which British subjects are kept in prison while their boxes are being tumbled out of the carriages.

After a week in Paris they are arguing about how to get to Baden. Alice has voted to go by Strasbourg.

'We will go by Strasbourg, then,' said Mr Palliser, gallantly.
'Not that I want to see that horrid church again,' said Glencora.
'Everything is alike horrid to you, I think,' said her husband. 'You are determined not to be contented, so that it matters very little which way we go.'
'That's the truth,' said his wife. 'It does matter very little.'

They went on to Baden – with very little delay at Strasbourg, and found half an hotel prepared for their reception. Here the carriage was brought into use for the first time, and the mistress of the carriage talked of sending home for Dandy and Flirt. Mr

Palliser, when he heard the proposition, calmly assured his wife that the horses would not bear the journey. 'They would be so out of condition,' he said, 'as not to be worth anything for two or three months.'

'I only meant to send for them if they could come in a balloon,' said Lady Glencora.

While Trollope was working in the Post Office he invented the red pillar-boxes for posting letters. No doubt many of his pillar-boxes have carried letters backing the successful claim of the Trollope Society for his inclusion in Poets' Corner. We might do worse than use them to support the claims of others; for instance his widowed mother, Frances, who indomitably manufactured novels by the dozen to keep her family in food and clothes. And why not two great masters of the English language, in poetry and prose, Pope and Carlyle?

Alexander Pope (1688–1744) was the son of a London linen-draper. Illness left him stunted at twelve, but he had the voice of 'a little nightingale'. There was little of the nightingale in his verse, which was brilliantly cerebral. Today, whenever we 'damn with faint praise', 'break a butterfly on the wheel' or 'rush in where angels fear to tread', we are consciously or unconsciously quoting Pope.

from: *An Essay on Man*

Know then thyself, presume not God to scan;
The proper study of Mankind is Man.

from: *Epigrams*

ON THE COLLAR OF A DOG WHICH I GAVE TO
HIS ROYAL HIGHNESS

I am his Highness' dog at Kew;
Pray tell me, sir, whose dog are you?

Nature and Nature's Laws lay hid in Night.
GOD said, *Let Newton be!* and all was Light.

Thomas Carlyle (1795–1881) was the son of a Scottish stonemason. His handsome, rough-hewn head and passion for philosophy made him a natural 'Sage of Chelsea', where he and his
brilliant wife, Jane Welsh, lived. He founded the famous London
Library. His defence of 'leadership' reduced his popularity after
Hitler's advent, but today his imaginative, if gothic prose is once
more beguiling, as seen in his *History of the French Revolution*.

'France was long a despotism tempered by epigrams.' 'A whiff of
grapeshot.' 'The seagreen Incorruptible' (on Robespierre).

and in *Heroes and Hero-Worship*

THE HERO AS POET

The *true* beautiful . . . differs from the *false*, as Heaven does from
Vauxhall.[1] . . .

Whoever looks intelligently at this Shakespeare may recognise
that he too was a *Prophet*, in his way; of an insight analogous to
the Prophetic, though he took it up in another strain . . . 'We are
such stuff as Dreams are made of!' That scroll in Westminster
Abbey, which few read with understanding, is of the depth of any
Seer. But the man sang; did not preach, except musically.

For good measure we might also post a letter on behalf of
Evelyn Waugh for his masterpiece *A Handful of Dust*. Another
strong candidate is that great English humorist, P. G. Wode-
house, whose Jeeves has given his name to a whole class of Englishmen, the gentleman's gentleman; remembering, however, that
it could be considered dangerous to let loose the author of *The
Great Sermon Handicap* in Westminster Abbey.

---

[1] Vauxhall Gardens were famous as a resort for pleasure and entertainment.

Strangely enough there seems to be a lack of modern religious poets in Poets' Corner. I would suggest the addition of Francis Thompson (1859–1907). Thompson spoke for the London poor, who slept beside him under the arches of Charing Cross, seeing Christ walking on the water, 'not of Gennesareth but Thames.' He was an opium addict, like Coleridge and Southey. Like all true poets he hated the changing lie and loved the unchanging truth:

> Wherefore should the singer sing,
>   So his song be true?
> Truth is ever old, old,
>   Song ever new.
>
> Ere the world was, was the lie,
>   And the truth too:
> But the old lie still is old,
>   The old truth new.

The absence of Robert Bridges (1844–1930) from Poets' Corner seems inexplicable, as I have already remarked. Bridges was deeply interested in experimental verse, influencing and publicising his great friend the poet Gerard Manley Hopkins, who, along with T. S. Eliot and Ezra Pound, was responsible for the development of modern poetry. Bridges' long *Testament of Beauty* is full of impressive passages; his hymn 'All My Hope on God is Founded' has passed the barrier of sects; his 'Nightingales' is among the many lovely lyrics written to that popular poetic bird:

> Beautiful must be the mountains whence ye come,
> And bright in the fruitful valleys the streams, wherefrom
> Ye learn your song:

Two other twentieth-century poets who are not yet in Poets' Corner have given us, among other things, some idea of how poetry works. W. H. Davies memorably challenged the active world:

> What is this life if full of care
> We have no time to stand and stare?

Poetry, he said, is not to be judged by the world of action:

> We poets pride ourselves on what
> We feel, and not what we achieve;
> The world may call our children fools,
> Enough for us that we conceive.

Walter de la Mare shows how the world that poets write *about* is transmuted and vanishes into their poetry. In his poem 'The Linnet' he imagines it singing in an exquisite world of bramble-sprays and harebells and thyme,

> As if this beauty and grace
> Did to one bird belong,
> And, at a flutter of wing
> Might vanish in song.

In making my selection of poetry and prose for this anthology, I have had to remember that I was commissioned by my publishers to make a personal choice. I really do like all the pieces that follow. None is included because I think it ought to be there; or because it appears in all the anthologies. That is not to say that many of my choices do not appear in other collections. There is such a thing as an agreed opinion on what is great poetry. One would expect an anthology of Poets' Corner to contain a large number of universal favourites.

My choices have been made in the light of various personal experiences. I cannot help liking, for instance, the poems that have been familiar to me since childhood. They may not always be the very best; but they do ring lustily in memory's ear. The narrative poems of Scott come into that category. And after learning to sing 'Ye banks and braes o' bonnie Doon' at school, I can have no doubt about my choice of at least one of Burns' great lyrics.

Another factor that has influenced my choice is also a personal one: I had met seven of the poets in question. The selections I have made from Gilbert Murray, John Masefield, T. S. Eliot, David Jones, Robert Graves, Edmund Blunden and Wystan

Auden (in chronological order of birth), seem to fit in with the impressions these poets made on me. Masefield's sea-blue eyes, for instance, that I watched as a schoolgirl during a poetry-speaking competition he was conducting, made sure that I chose something from his 'Salt-Water Ballads', however hackneyed. Or again, Auden doubtless came to reject his poem 'Spain' (as indeed he rejected all writing of poetry compared with the duty to love God and our neighbour), but it is 'Spain' that represents the Auden I knew.

The selection of poems from another category – the Romantics – I found at once easy and difficult. On the whole I would say that this is the period of Eng. Lit. that means most to me. Never mind that it is now seen to be 'subjective' with perhaps undue emphasis on individual feelings. Wordsworth, Coleridge, Byron, Shelley, Keats have been with me for over seventy years. I know a good many of their poems by heart. The first poetry book I ever bought (at 14) was an illustrated edition of Coleridge's *The Rime of the Ancient Mariner*. The first poetry books I asked for as birthday or Christmas presents were Milton's *Comus* illustrated by Arthur Rackham, and Keats' complete works, leather-bound in rosy red. So I have had some difficulty in picking out the limited number of fifty or sixty lines that I could give to Keats. For a time I found it absolutely impossible to choose between his 'Ode to a Nightingale' and 'Ode on a Grecian Urn'. In the end I decided that the essence of the latter could be caught in a few supreme stanzas, whereas the incomparable 'Nightingale' needed more lines of quotation than I could afford, in order to capture its unique atmosphere.

I had similar problems over Byron's lyrics – I wanted them all – though his *Don Juan*, being associated with my middle age rather than my youth, was easier to deal with. I decided to go for a stanza that did justice to his funny, astringent side, rather than his romanticism. My choices of Wordsworth were firmly fixed by visits to the 'Wordsworth country': reading aloud 'Tintern Abbey' *in situ*, and other poems in places where he had lived. Shelley in a sense presented me with the least of my problems. I could never forget the effect of first reading his *Prometheus Unbound*. This poem, together with Shakespeare's *Hamlet*, gave me the same kind of thrill as Keats felt on first looking into Chapman's Homer. So I had to have a passage from it. After that, I rather unhappily discarded Shelley's 'To Night' in preference to other favourites. At one point I had toyed with the mad idea of including in my anthology every single poem written by poets on one of their own favourite subjects: nightingales.

Shakespeare was not exactly a problem, more an impossibility. His mini-biography seemed as hard to deal with as the selections from his poetry. At another mad moment I thought of omitting his somewhat mysterious CV altogether, so much of it is speculative, so little of it known with certainty. As Thomas Hardy wrote in his poem, 'To Shakespeare – After Three Hundred Years':

> Bright baffling soul, least capturable of themes,
> Thou, who display'dst a life of commonplace
> Leaving no intimate word or personal trace.

At first I considered simply introducing our greatest genius with tributes from his fellow poets through the centuries. Of course this did not work; and in any case it would have spoilt my attempt to achieve a positive structure for the anthology. In making my selection from Shakespeare's plays and poems, however, I have had to introduce a principle that did not operate at all among the minor poets and only to some extent among the major ones. This was the decision to give up sifting favourites – there were far too many in Shakespeare – and to attempt a demonstration of Shakespeare's varied and extensive genius. Hence songs, a sonnet and speeches.

With some of the seventeenth- and eighteenth-century 'minimal' poets, the problem has not been to select from too many favourites but to find something that seemed to me at all interesting or quotable. The one play by Francis Beaumont, for instance, that is thought to be entirely his own work, *The Knight of the Burning Pestle*, involved me in quite a struggle. At last it yielded a passage that I hoped came up to scratch. But when I tested it on a poet friend, she said she could not make anything of it. So I added Beaumont's epitaph on the Abbey tombs; it is not certain that Beaumont was the author, but at any rate it is intelligible and highly evocative. In the words of the poet Arthur Hugh Clough (and how I wish he were uttering them in Poets' Corner) 'Say not the struggle nought availeth . . .'

Many anthologies of poetry have done without any biographical details whatever. Some do not even give dates – and if the poets are arranged in alphabetical order it may be a little disconcerting to find Siegfried Sassoon preceding Shakespeare, and Shakespeare immediately followed by Shelley; the two hundred years between them having somehow rolled away. I find it uncomfortable, as a reader, to have to adjust to such a frequent clash of periods. In the case of an anthology based on Poets' Corner, the marble figures and terse epitaphs (some in Latin) seem to cry out for 'brief lives' to round off and clarify this sometimes confusing pantheon. I have aimed to keep each 'brief life' in my anthology to a little more than one hundred words. This was a necessity of space. I must explain, however, that it is not always a major poet who requires the longest 'brief life'. Some of the minor poets or playwrights who are today almost unknown, seem to need a few extra words to bring them to life.

Perhaps I should recall at this point what is obvious to anyone who has ever stood in Poets' Corner – that the Corner is really a pantheon for *artists*. Though predominantly devoted to literature, there is to be found in it the glorious musician George Frederick Handel, complete with trumpet, score, organ pipes and heavenly harp and harpist; the actors Garrick, Irving and, since his recent death, Olivier; the architect Robert Adam; a doctor, Joshua Ward, an 'artist' in quack medicines; the orator John Campbell, 2nd Duke of Argyll; the singer Jenny Lind; and Sir Richard Coxe the 'Taster' to Queen Elizabeth I, presumably a master of the culinary arts, with a special nose for health foods and poisons. Quite a number of pure politicians have slipped in, with no claims to artistry. And there are some saintly or sadistic clergymen, from the fourteenth-century Abbot Nicholas de Lytlington, who out of his own resources built the wonderful Jerusalem Chamber, to the seventeenth-century Dr Busby, headmaster of Westminster School and a 'whipper'. Adam Fox, a canon of Westminster, was a minor poet who wrote hymns and was Professor of Poetry at Oxford.

I come finally to the pleasant business of giving thanks. Three famous writers of the past have made my task enjoyable through their wit, humour and profundity. John Aubrey (1626–1697) has the gift in his *Brief Lives* of raising every subject he touches to new, sometimes bizarre heights. We do not always have to believe every one of his colourful details: that Shakespeare's father was a butcher and that his helpful son made a speech after every chop; or that Milton was of so 'chearfull' a humour that 'even in his Gowte-fits' he would sing. But Aubrey's critical essays do wonders for those parts of writers that other critics do not reach. Often he would give a physical description of his subject, an all too rare custom. John Denham, for example, had hair that 'was but thin and flaxen, with a moiste curle'. Denham liked student jokes and once inked out all the street signs from Temple Bar to Charing Cross. 'This I had', wrote Aubrey, 'from R. Estcott, Esq., that carried the Inke-pott.' After trouble with his young and beautiful second wife, Denham went mad for a time, informing Charles II that he, Denham, was the Holy Ghost.

My other historical authorities are of course Dr Samuel Johnson, whose *Lives of the Poets* is an evergreen miracle of good sense and paradox; and Macaulay for his vibrant and amusing *Essays*.

Having discharged my debt to these brilliant writers of the past, I wish to thank the editors of modern anthologies and reference books, to which I owe so much extended pleasure and so many short cuts. Among the anthologies, Jill Balcon's elegant and moving little volume, *The Pity of War*, stands out. It is devoted to the sixteen poets of the Great War who are remembered together in Poets' Corner. Other anthologies include *Poems of To-day* ('to-day' being the era of the Georgians), Palgrave's *Golden Treasury* and its *Silver* sequel, and the many *Oxford* books of verse. Among reference books, the two most essential were Margaret Drabble's new edition of *The Oxford Companion to English Literature* (always reliable and often entertaining) and the many-volumed *Dictionary of National Biography*.

Without the London Library I should have been nowhere. Its bookstacks are more challenging than any maze, its Reading Room is more comfortable than any club in Pall Mall, and its staff are as expeditious as if they were trying to sell books during a recession, instead of just lending them. I am also most grateful to the staff of the British Library (Manuscripts section) and to my local Chelsea Public Library. I am greatly indebted to the authors or editors of biographies or *Collected Poems* or *Works*, and I hope I have remembered all of them and their publishers in my Acknowledgments.

In an anthology like this, first thoughts are not always best. I still think I was right to create, by my choices, an overall atmosphere that was observably related to the great building of which Poets' Corner is a part. That meant my choosing a number of lovely, and even encouraging poems about death. But as time went on, a danger developed of the tone becoming too die-away and melancholy. I have since tried to remedy this, but without attempting to achieve an academic balance, or to dissect the works I have chosen. Poetry predominates over prose among writers who have excelled in both, for after all this is, nominally at least, *Poets'* Corner. But I would not have chosen Hardy's or the Brontë sisters' poems, for instance, if I had not enjoyed reading them for years past. I have tried to give all this marble, slate and bronze a voice. My hope would be that others might, as a result, re-read some of these poems, novels and plays, imagining their own anthologies.

CAEDMON

(*c.* AD 670)

The Venerable Bede (AD 673–735), *monk and scholar, is our authority on Caedmon. He was said to have been a simple peasant serving the monastery of Whitby, who saw in a vision his vocation to write sacred verse in English – Latin, the usual medium, would have been impossible for him. He is therefore the first of several verse makers in Poets' Corner who have been named 'father' of English poetry. He put the Scriptures into English and also wrote, so far as we know, one original poem.*

Hymn of Creation

Dorothy Whitelock's translation in her The Beginnings of English Society.

> Now we must praise the guardian of the heavenly kingdom,
> the powers of the Creator and his thoughts,
> the works of the Father of glory,
> as he, the eternal Lord,
> appointed the beginning of every wondrous thing;
> he, the holy lord, the Guardian of mankind,
> first created for the children of men
> the heaven as a roof.
> Then the eternal Lord, Ruler Almighty,
> afterwards adorned the world,
> the earth, for men.

The first four lines in the original Old English. There is no rhyme, but alliteration and a caesura – pause – in each line.

> Nu scylum hergan hefaenricaes uard,
> metudaes maecti end his modgidanc,
> uerc uuldurfadur, sue he uundra gihuaes,
> eci dryctin, or astelidae; . . .

GEOFFREY CHAUCER

(*c.* 1340–1400)

In Chaucer we have a second 'father of English poetry', Caedmon being the first. From French and Italian literature Chaucer learnt many new uses of verse, including romance, satire and comedy. He adapted well-known stories to his own purposes, as Shakespeare was to do two hundred years later. The son of a London vintner, Chaucer chose an inn – the Tabard – appropriately enough for the starting point of his most famous tales. All his life he was in touch with the court: appointed page to a son of Edward III; taken prisoner in the French wars and ransomed with the help of Edward; married to the sister of John of Gaunt's third wife. The pilgrims of his The Canterbury Tales *are living rather than stylised people, their individuality heightened by dialogue and digression. Their* Tales *may be haunted by magic and legend but they themselves come from the real world.*

from: *The Canterbury Tales*

THE WIFE OF BATH'S TALE

Thoughts on marriage and women, translated from the fourteenth-century English by Nevill Coghill.

> 'Now it so happened, I began to say,
> Long, long ago in good King Arthur's day.
> There was a knight who was a lusty liver.
> One day as he came riding from the river
> He saw a maiden walking all forlorn
> Ahead of him, alone as she was born.
> And of that maiden, spite of all she said,
> By very force he took her maidenhead.'

The knight, condemned to death, is granted a reprieve by King Arthur on one condition: that he answer a question put to him by the Queen, within one year and one day.

'"What is the thing that women most desire?
Beware the axe and say as I require."

'He knocked at every house, searched every place,
Yes, anywhere that offered hope of grace.
What could it be that women wanted most?
But all the same he never touched a coast,
Country or town in which there seemed to be
Any two people willing to agree.'

*'Honour', 'jollity', 'clothes', 'fun in bed', 'flattery', 'many marriages' –
which? At last his time is up.*

'As he rode home in a dejected mood
Suddenly, at the margin of a wood,
He saw a dance upon the leafy floor
Of four and twenty ladies, nay, and more.
Eagerly he approached, in hope to learn
Some words of wisdom ere he should return;
But lo! Before he came to where they were,
Dancers and dance all vanished into air!
There wasn't a living creature to be seen
Save one old woman crouched upon the green.
A fouler-looking creature I suppose
Could scarcely be imagined. She arose
And said, "Sir knight, there's no way on from here.
Tell me what you are looking for, my dear,
For peradventure that were best for you;
We old, old women know a thing or two."
"Dear Mother," said the knight, "alack the day!
I am as good as dead if I can't say
What thing it is that women most desire;
If you could tell me I would pay your hire."'

*She makes him promise to do whatever she requires of him in return
for her information.*

'And then she crooned her gospel in his ear
And told him to be glad and not to fear.'

On the very last day the knight replies to the Queen.

> ' "My liege and lady, in general," said he,
> "A woman wants the self-same sovereignty
> Over her husband as over her lover,
> And master him; he must not be above her.
> That is your greatest wish, whether you kill
> Or spare me; please yourself. I wait your will." '

The knight is spared; but at what a price! The foul old crone asks him to marry her.

> 'Great was the anguish churning in his head
> When he and she were piloted to bed;
> He wallowed back and forth in desperate style.
> His ancient wife lay smiling all the while;
> At last she said, "Bless us! Is this, my dear,
> How knights and wives get on together here? . . .
> You're carrying on as if you were half-witted.
> Say, for God's love, what sin have I committed?" '

He explains that she is low-bred, poor and old, to which she retorts –

> ' " 'Gentle is he that does a gentle deed.' . . .
> He who accepts his poverty unhurt
> I'd say is rich although he lacked a shirt.
> But truly poor are they who whine and fret
> And covet what they cannot hope to get. . . .
> Lastly you taxed me, sir, with being old.
> Yet even if you never had been told
> By ancient books, you gentlemen engage
> Yourselves in honour to respect old age." '

Finally she gives him a choice: to have her old, ugly and loyal, or young, pretty and – you know what . . . The knight at last gives the right reply: 'You make the choice yourself,' he groans.

> ' "Kiss me," she cried. "No quarrels! On my oath
> And word of honour you shall find me both,

That is, both fair and faithful as a wife; ...
Cast up the curtain, husband, Look at me!"
    And when indeed the knight had looked to see,
Lo, she was young and lovely, rich in charms.
In ecstasy he caught her in his arms,
His heart went bathing in a bath of blisses,
And melted in a hundred thousand kisses,
And she responded in the fullest measure
With all that could delight or give him pleasure.
    So they lived ever after to the end
In perfect bliss; and may Christ Jesus send
Us husbands meek and young and fresh in bed,
And grace to overbid them when we wed.
And – Jesu hear my prayer! – cut short the lives
Of those who won't be governed by their wives.'

WILLIAM CAMDEN

(1551–1623)

*Headmaster of Westminster School, Camden is perhaps the most creative
of that learned breed. By the age of thirty-five he had become an antiquarian and published his famous* Britannia: or, a Chorographical
Description of the Flourishing Kingdoms of England, Scotland
and Ireland, and the Islands Adjacent, from the Earliest Antiquity.
*It was translated from the Latin by Richard Gough in 1806. Thirty-two
years later Camden's admirers founded the Camden Society to do for
the British Empire what Camden had done for Britain.* Britannia *is a
lively mixture of antiquarian history, legend, 'modern' history, guide-
book with maps and illustrations, and forerunner to* Debrett.

from: *Ireland*

Part of Britannia, *translated by Gough. Camden is basing his account on that of a priest called Gabriel Goodman, Dean of Westminster, and the Welsh historian Giraldus Cambrensis.*

THE ANCIENT AND MODERN MANNERS OF THE
'WILD' OR NATIVE IRISH

In general this people are robust and remarkably nimble, of bold and haughty spirits, sharp witted, lively, warlike, prodigal of life, patient of want, heat and cold, of an amorous complexion, hospitable to strangers, constant in their attachments, implacable in their resentments, credulous, greedy for glory, impatient of reproach and injuries, and, as Giraldus formerly represented them, 'violent in all their passions; no people worse than the bad among them, nor better than the good.'

Such is the account my author gives of the manners of the wild Irish. In the rest, and almost all who inhabit what is called the English Pale, there is nothing wanting that makes a part of cultivation and humanity.

A rather different picture of ancient Ireland, written by Saint Donatus, Bishop of Etruria, (died 840), and quoted by Camden.

> Her fruitful soil for ever teems with wealth
> With gems her waters, and her air with health;
> Her verdant fields with milk and honey flow;
> Her woolly fleeces vie with virgin snow;
> Her waving furrows float with bearded corn,
> And arms and arts her envied sons adorn.
> No savage bear with lawless fury roves,
> No raging lion through her sacred groves;
> No poison there infects, no scaly snake
> Creeps through the grass, nor frog annoys the lake.
> An island worthy of its pious race,
> In war triumphant, and unmatched in peace.

EDMUND SPENSER

(c. 1552–1599)

Though Spenser wrote of 'merry London, my most kindly nurse', he was proud to be connected with the Spencers of Althorp, Northampton-shire. A Renaissance man who studied the poets of Greece and Italy yet created a native English muse, Spenser counted among his friends other Renaissance men – Sidney, Leicester, Essex. As for that astute Machi-avellian monarch Elizabeth I, she was his Gloriana, his Fairy Queen. Spenser served the Crown in rebellious Ireland and in 1598 his home, Kilcolman, was burnt down. He died a few months later in London. The philosophy of Renaissance Man idealised the ruling race and saw nothing for the Irish but suppression. However, the mother-of-pearl loveliness of Spenser's imagery, and his gentle 'Spenserian stanza', pre-sented the harsh realities of the sixteenth century in a seductive new light.

from: The Faerie Queene

THE LEGEND OF THE RED CROSS KNIGHT
CANTO I

The Lady Una has warned the knight against entering 'Error's den' in 'the wandering wood'.

> But full of fire and greedy hardiment
>   The youthful knight could not for ought be stayed,
>   But forth unto the darksome hole he went,
>   And lookèd in: his glistering armour made
>   A little gloomy light, much like a shade,
>   By which he saw the ugly monster plain,
>   Half like a serpent horribly displayed,
>   But th'other half did woman's shape retain,
> Most loathsome, filthy, foul and full of vile disdain.

from: *Prothalamion*

OR A SPOUSALL VERSE MADE BY EDM. SPENSER IN HONOUR OF THE
DOUBLE MARRIAGE OF THE LADY ELIZABETH AND THE LADY
KATHERINE SOMERSET 1596

Calm was the day, and through the trembling air,
Sweet breathing Zephyrus did softly play
A gentle spirit, that lightly did delay
Hot Titan's beams, which then did glister fair:
When I whom sullen care,
Through discontent of my long fruitless stay
In Prince's Court, and expectation vain
Of idle hopes which still do fly away,
Like empty shadows, did afflict my brain,
Walked forth to ease my pain
Along the shore of silver streaming Thames,
Whose rutty banks, the which his river hems,
Was painted all with variable flowers,
And all the meads adorned with dainty gems,
Fit to deck maidens' bowers,
And crown their paramours,[1]
Against the bridal day, which is not long;
   Sweet Thames run softly, till I end my song.

ISAAC CASAUBON

(1559–1614)

*Writing entirely in Greek-besprinkled Renaissance Latin, Casaubon is
rarely studied today, even by the successors of those classical and ecclesiastical scholars whom he impressed so deeply, 400 years ago, with his
learned commentaries. Born in Geneva, Casaubon gradually lost his
belief in the Calvinism of his Huguenot refugee parents. He held*

---

[1] Bridegrooms, rather than lovers.

*academic posts in Geneva and Montpelier; then Paris, perhaps tempor-
arily attracted to Rome. Visiting London in 1610, he became naturalised
English the following year (without speaking English or understanding
the currency) and was given a pension by James I, whose (Anglican)
faith seemed at last to suit the deeply religious Casaubon.*

A proud boast in a letter from Casaubon to Baudius (translated).

It is not the manner of the English to import distinguished men
of learning from other countries.

*Casaubon had been invited over by the Archbishop of Canterbury
himself.*

*Casaubon had 'a curiosity for marvels'. Hearing of a baby that had been
rescued supernaturally from a house on fire, its cradle 'powdered with
crosses', Casaubon wrote to his informant:*

I received lately two letters from you. The first transformed me
wholly into wonder; without doubt the thing you write of is
miraculous; but whence, I cannot affirm.

Part of Casaubon's Will, 21 June 1614.

As for my goods which the Lord hath lent me, which I shall leave
the day of my decease, my will is that my debts which shall be
found lawful shall be paid ... [*After leaving gifts, including 30
crowns and 'four of my greatest books' among the Library of the French
Church in London, the French Church itself and the poor of his parish,
he appoints his wife sole executor, leaving her half his estate.*] As for
the other half which shall remain, I will not that my son John
Casaubon have any part thereof but only one Cup of the value of
30 crowns [*John had a convert's pension, having become a Roman
Catholic.*] ... Item, I will and ordain that each one of my daughters
have 200 crowns, which being done, my meaning is that the whole
remnant be equally divided among my sons and daughters [*except
that the son most fitted to 'sustain' the family shall also get 'the Cup of
Mr Scaliger', the greatest Renaissance scholar and critic in the same
line as Casaubon*].

MICHAEL DRAYTON

(1563–1631)

Drayton was born in the year before Shakespeare and in the same part of the English Midlands (Warwickshire) but even less is known of his personal life than of Shakespeare's. His burial in the Abbey was probably due to three factors: the sheer volume of his writing – not always a recommendation today; some individual patriotic poems such as the 'Ballad of Agincourt' with its striking first line, 'Fair stood the wind for France'; and the generosity of one of his patrons, Lady Anne Clifford, Countess of Dorset, who paid for his fine tomb, since he died without means. But today no tomb seems too fine for the author of one of the most moving love poems in the language.

from: *Sonnets to Idea*
IV, 1619

'Idea' was probably Anne Polesworth, daughter of his employer.

Since there's no help, come let us kiss and part.
Nay, I have done; you get no more of me,
And I am glad, yea, glad with all my heart,
That thus so cleanly I myself can free;
Shake hands for ever, cancel all our vows,
And when we meet at any time again,
Be it not seen in either of our brows
That we one jot of former love retain.
Now at the last gasp of Love's latest breath,
When, his pulse failing, Passion speechless lies,
When Faith is kneeling by his bed of death,
And Innocence is closing up his eyes,
   Now if thou wouldst, when all have given him over,
   From death to life thou mightst him yet recover.

WILLIAM SHAKESPEARE

(1564–1616)

Shakespeare's father was a glover; his mother, Mary Arden, introduced a higher social strain. Baptised and educated in his birthplace, Stratford-upon-Avon, he married Anne Hathaway, though eight years her junior, and they had three children, the eldest a six-months' baby. He may have begun his career as a country schoolmaster. First mentioned as an actor at twenty-eight, he was said by a rival to consider himself 'the only Shakescene' who could 'bombast out' blank verse on the London stage. He was to work with the Globe Theatre company for most of his active life, writing much of the 'bombast' that brought them fame. Meanwhile his father, now a JP, bought himself into the 'gentry' class; William acquired a substantial house, New Place, Stratford. William died on the same day and month as he was believed to have been born – 23 April. With the death of his only granddaughter in 1670, the family died out. But the 'Sweet Swan of Avon', as Ben Jonson called him, was never to sing a swan song; he remained 'not of an age, but for all time'.

from: *A Midsummer Night's Dream*
ACT II SCENE ONE

I know a bank whereon the wild thyme blows,
Where oxlip and the nodding violet grows
Quite over-canopied with luscious woodbine,
With sweet musk-roses, and with eglantine;
There sleeps Titania some time of the night,
Lull'd in these flowers with dances and delight;
And there the snake throws her enamell'd skin,
Weed wide enough to wrap a fairy in.

from: *King Lear*
ACT V SCENE TWO

EDGAR What, in ill thoughts again? Men must endure
Their going hence, even as their coming hither:
Ripeness is all.

ACT V SCENE THREE

[*To Cordelia*]

LEAR No, no, no, no! let's away to prison;
We two alone will sing like birds i' the cage;
When thou dost ask me blessing, I'll kneel down
And ask of thee forgiveness; so we'll live,
And pray, and sing, and tell old tales, and laugh
At gilded butterflies, and hear poor rogues
Talk of court news; and we'll talk with them too,
Who loses, and who wins; who's in and who's out;
And take upon us the mystery of things,
As if we were God's spies: and we'll wear out;
In a wall'd prison, packs and sects of great ones
That ebb and flow by the moon.

from: *Cymbeline*
ACT IV SCENE TWO

Fear no more the heat o' the sun,
    Nor the furious winter's rages,
Thou thy worldly task hast done,
    Home art gone, and ta'en thy wages:
Golden lads and girls all must,
As chimney-sweepers come to dust.

from: *The Tempest*
ACT IV SCENE ONE

Our revels now are ended. These our actors,
As I foretold you, were all spirits, and
Are melted into air, into thin air:

And, like the baseless fabric of this vision,
The cloud-capp'd towers, the gorgeous palaces,
The solemn temples, the great globe itself,
Yea, all which it inherit, shall dissolve,
And, like this insubstantial pageant faded,
Leave not a rack behind. We are such stuff
As dreams are made on; and our little life
Is rounded with a sleep.

Sonnet (116)

Let me not to the marriage of true minds
Admit impediments. Love is not love
Which alters when it alteration finds,
Or bends with the remover to remove:
O, no! it is an ever fixèd mark,
That looks on tempests and is never shaken;
It is the star to every wandering bark,
Whose worth's unknown, although his height be taken.
Love's not Time's fool, though rosy lips and cheeks
Within his bending sickle's compass come;
Love alters not with his brief hours and weeks,
But bears it out even to the edge of doom.
    If this be error and upon me proved,
    I never writ, nor no man ever loved.

BEN JONSON

(c. 1573–1637)

The posthumous son of a London clergyman, the gifted boy was educated at Westminster and Cambridge. From Border forbears may have come his combative spirit. By twenty-five he had twice killed his man, suffered imprisonment, and had a play put on at the Curtain in which his admired friend Will Shakespeare acted. He produced masques with Inigo Jones, though they later quarrelled. In effect he was the first poet laureate; he was honoured by Oxford University and ardently admired by James I, and by his noble patrons and poetic disciples. He was smitten by the accidental burning of his library (he blamed Vulcan, the god of fire) and a stroke, but his end was remarkable: he was buried standing on his feet in the nave of the Abbey with the monumental inscription, 'O rare Ben Jonson'. According to one story, Jonson felt too poor for a full-length tomb: '2 by 2 feet will do for all I want.' 'You shall have it,' said the Dean.

Epigram: To the Reader

Pray thee, take care, that tak'st my book in hand,
To read it well; that is, to understand.

Epigram: To Fool or Knave

Thy praise or dispraise is to me alike;
One doth not stroke me, nor the other strike.

from: THE FOREST

To Celia

Drink to me only with thine eyes,
    And I will pledge with mine;
Or leave a kiss but in the cup,
    And I'll not look for wine.
The thirst that from the soul doth rise
    Doth ask a drink divine;
But might I of Jove's nectar sup,
    I would not change for thine.

Epitaph on the Countess of Pembroke

Underneath this sable hearse
Lies the subject of all verse,

Sidney's sister, Pembroke's mother;
Death! ere thou hast slain another,
Learn'd and fair, and good as she,
Time shall throw a dart at thee.

from: *A Pindaric Ode*

TO THE IMMORTAL MEMORY AND FRIENDSHIP OF THAT NOBLE
PAIR, SIR LUCIUS CARY AND SIR H. MORISON

It is not growing like a tree
In bulk, doth make men better be;
Or standing long an oak, three hundred year,
To fall a log at last, dry, bald, and sear:
A lily of a day,
Is fairer far in May,
Although it fall and die that night
It was the plant and flower of light.
In small proportions we just beauties see;
And in short measures, life may perfect be.

 # FRANCIS & JOHN BEAUMONT

(c. 1584–1616/1583–1627)

Descended from an old family and born in Leicestershire, Francis Beaumont turned to drama in preference to his father's legal profession. Collaborating with John Fletcher in the writing of fifteen plays, he was almost certainly the sole author of The Knight of the Burning Pestle, *a comedy which has features of pantomime and farce. Beaumont's career as an active playwright was brought to a prosperous close by marriage to a wealthy wife, and the amenities of a home in Kent. Fifty years ago, 'Beaumont and Fletcher' were always spoken of together, as if they were an inseparable partnership, like 'Fortnum and Mason' or 'Marks and Spencer'; but modern scholarship now distinguishes them. Strangely enough, instead of John Fletcher being Francis Beaumont's partner on the gravestone in Poets' Corner, it is Francis's brother Sir John Beaumont, whose poetry, incidentally, gets no mention either in the* Dictionary of National Biography *or in* The Oxford Companion to English Literature, *though a charming elegy on his seven-year-old son appears in* The New Oxford Book of English Verse.

FRANCIS BEAUMONT

from: *The Knight of the Burning Pestle*
ACT III SCENE ONE

A duet sung by the lovers Jasper and Luce.

JASP   Tell me, dearest, what is love?
LUCE   'Tis a lightning from above;
       'Tis an arrow, 'tis a fire;
       'Tis a boy they call Desire;
         'Tis a smile
         Doth beguile
JASP   The poor hearts of men that prove.

       Tell me more, are women true?
LUCE   Some love change, and so do you.
JASP   Are they fair and never kind?
LUCE   Yes, when men turn with the wind.
JASP   Are they froward?
LUCE   Ever toward
       Those that love, to love anew.

The comic element in the play depends mainly on the interventions of a Citizen – a city grocer – and his Wife from the audience. They insist on their apprentice, Ralph, taking part in the performance, and eventually they change the plot in order to get Ralph onto the stage more often. Ralph is 'the Knight of the Burning Pestle' – the grocer's lad.

—{ 50 }—

[*Enter Mistress Merrythought.*]

CITIZENS WIFE [*to her husband, interrupting the play*] Look, George, here comes Mistress Merrythought again! and I would have Ralph come and fight with the giant; I tell you true, I long to see't.

CITIZEN Good Mistress Merrythought, begone, I pray you, for my sake; I pray you, forbear a little; you shall have audience presently; I have a little business.

WIFE Mistress Merrythought, if it please you to refrain your passion a little, till Ralph have despatched the giant out of the way, we shall think ourselves much bound to you. [*Exit Mistress Merrythought.*] I thank you, good Mistress Merrythought.

CITIZEN Boy, come hither. [*Enter Boy.*] Send away Ralph and this whoreson giant quickly.

BOY In good faith, sir, we cannot; you'll utterly spoil our play, and make it to be hissed; and it cost money; you will not suffer us to go on with our plot. – I pray, gentlemen, rule him.

CITIZEN Let him come now and despatch this, and I'll trouble you no more.

BOY Will you give me your hand of that?

WIFE Give him thy hand, George, do; and I'll kiss him. I warrant thee the youth means plainly.

BOY I'll send him to you presently.

On the Tombs in Westminster Abbey

> Mortality, behold, and fear,
> What a change of flesh is here!
> Think how many royal bones
> Sleep within this heap of stones,
> Hence removed from beds of ease,
> Dainty fare, and what might please,
> Fretted roofs, and costly shows,
> To a roof that flats the nose: . . .

For here they lie had realms and lands,
That now want strength to stir their hands;
Where from their pulpits sealed with dust
They preach: 'In greatness is no trust'.
Here's an acre sown indeed
With the richest royalest seed,
That the earth did e'er suck in
Since the first man died for sin. . . .
Here are sands (ignoble things)
Dropped from the ruined sides of kings;
With whom the poor man's earth being shown
The difference is not easily known.

SIR JOHN BEAUMONT

Of My Dear Son, Gervase Beaumont

Can I, who have for others oft compiled
The songs of Death, forget my sweetest child,
Which, like a flower crushed, with a blast is dead,
And ere full time hangs down his smiling head,
Expecting with clear hope to live anew
Among the angels, fed with heavenly dew?
We have this sign of joy, that many days,
While on the earth his struggling spirit stays,
The name of Jesus in his mouth contains
His only food, his sleep, his ease from pains. . . .
Dear Lord, receive my son, whose winning love
To me was like a friendship, far above
The course of nature or his tender age,
Whose looks could all my bitter griefs assuage;
Let his pure soul ordained seven years to be
In that frail body, which was part of me,
Remain my pledge in Heaven, as sent to show
How to this port at every step I go.

THOMAS TRIPLET

(1603–1670)

Now a long-forgotten divine, Triplet was educated at St Paul's School and Christ Church, Oxford. He took holy orders but was dispossessed of his preferments under the Commonwealth. They were restored to him in 1660 and he finally became Sub-Dean and Canon of Westminster, leaving £20 a year to four poor scholars of the school. Meanwhile, during the years of sequestration, he set up a school of his own. Dr Triplet adored honey and was once asked by a daring pupil for a taste of his store. Furious, Triplet kicked him downstairs. His own headmaster at St Paul's, Dr Gill, was a notorious 'whipper'. He beat Triplet, who revenged himself by persuading a friend to sing a ribald ballad under Gill's window. John Aubrey, author of the Brief Lives, *predicted that the ballad would outlive all Triplet's sermons.*

Ballad

A Frenchman void of English
Enquiring for Paul's steeple
His Pardonnez-moy
He[1] counted a toy,[2]
For he whipp't him before all the people.

For a piece of beef and turnip,
Neglected,[3] with a cabbage,
He took up the pillion
Of his bouncing maid Jillian,
And sous't her like a baggage.

---

[1] Gill.
[2] Trifling.
[3] Neglected by his maid.

WILLIAM DAVENANT

(1606–1668)

Son of an Oxford innkeeper, Davenant was said by Aubrey to be Shakespeare's natural child; Shakespeare would stay at the inn on his journeys between London and Stratford and give young William 'a hundred kisses'. At twenty-one Davenant had his first play performed, but his youth was blighted by ill health when, again according to Aubrey, he suffered a severe set-back with 'a terrible clap . . . which cost him his nose'. During the Civil War he became a Cavalier poet, was knighted by Charles I and organised royalist supplies, visiting Paris. Milton was said to have got him released when he was imprisoned. He lived to become an innovating playwright and producer, introducing scenery and women actresses to the stage. Succeeding Ben Jonson as de facto laureate, he also received a memorial that imitated Jonson's: 'O rare Will Davenant'.

from: *Ode in Remembrance of*
Master William Shakespeare

Beware, delighted poets, when you sing
To welcome nature in the early spring,
   Your numerous feet not tread
The banks of Avon; for each flower
As it ne'er knew a sun or shower
   Hangs there, the pensive head. . . .

The piteous river wept itself away
Long since, alas, to such a swift decay
   That, reach the map, and look
If you a river there can spy,
And for a river your mocked eye
   Will find a shallow brook.

Song
TO HIS MISTRESS

The lark now leaves his watery nest
 And climbing, shakes his dewy wings;
He takes this window for the East;
 And to implore your light, he sings,
Awake, awake, the morn will never rise,
Till she can dress her beauty at your eyes.

The merchant bows unto the seaman's star,
 The ploughman from the sun his season takes;
But still the lover wonders what they are,
 Who look for day before his mistress wakes.
Awake, awake, break through your veils of lawn!
Then draw your curtains, and begin the dawn.

The Soldier Going to the Field
TO HIS MISTRESS

Preserve thy sighs, unthrifty girl!
 To purify the air;
Thy tears to thread instead of pearl
 On bracelets of thy hair.

The trumpet makes the echo hoarse,
 And wakes the louder drum;
Expense of grief gains no remorse,
 When sorrow should be dumb.

For I must go where lazy peace
 Will hide her drowsy head;
And for the sport of kings, increase
 The number of the dead.

JOHN MILTON

(1608–1674)

Milton's life began in Bread Street, London, and divides into three parts. First, he studied and wrote poetry, including Comus *and* Lycidas. *Second, he moved 'to fresh woods and pastures new' when he became totally blind; with the help of secretaries, he performed the work of Latin Secretary and pamphleteer to the Parliament's Council of State. Third, after Charles II's Restoration, he began producing his greatest poetical works. Widowed twice and married three times, he had three daughters by his first wife who were to serve as his busy secretaries. 'They also serve who only stand and wait', he wrote of his blindness; however, Milton's moral critics might argue that his hard-worked daughters would gladly have spent more time just standing around.*

from: *Comus*
SONG

(To the water-nymph.)

> Sabrina fair
>   Listen where thou art sitting
> Under the glassy, cool, translucent wave,
>   In twisted braids of lilies knitting
> The loose train of thy amber-dropping hair;
>   Listen for dear honour's sake,
>   Goddess of the silver lake,
>   Listen and save.

from: *Paradise Lost*
BOOK I

Of Man's first disobedience and the fruit
Of that forbidden tree, whose mortal taste
Brought death into the world and all our woe,

With loss of Eden, till one greater Man
Restore us and regain the blissful seat,
Sing heav'nly Muse.

Satan's welcome to Hell.

Farewell happy fields,
Where joy for ever dwells! hail horrors! hail
Infernal world; and thou profoundest hell
Receive thy new possessor; one who brings
A mind not to be changed by place or time:
The mind is its own place, and in itself
Can make a heav'n of hell, a hell of heav'n.
What matter where, if I be still the same,
And what I should be, all but less than He
Whom thunder hath made greater? Here at least
We shall be free; th' Almighty hath not built
Here for his envy, will not drive us hence:
Here we may reign secure, and in my choice
To reign is worth ambition, though in hell:
Better to reign in hell, than serve in heav'n.

BOOK XII

Adam and Eve are driven from Eden.

High in front advanced,
The brandished sword of God before them blazed
Fierce as a comet; which with torrid heat,
And vapour as the Lydian air adust,
Began to parch that temperate clime: whereat
In either hand the hast'ning angel caught
Our ling'ring parents, and to the eastern gate
Led them direct, and down the cliff as fast
To the subjected plain; then disappeared.

They looking back all th' eastern side beheld
Of Paradise, so late their happy seat,
With dreadful faces thronged and fiery arms:
Waved over by that flaming brand; the gate
With dreadful faces thronged and fiery arms.
Some natural tears they dropped, but wiped them soon:
The world was all before them, where to choose
Their place of rest, and Providence their guide.
They, hand in hand, with wand'ring steps and slow,
Through Eden took their solitary way.

Sonnet
ON HIS BLINDNESS

When I consider how my light is spent,
   Ere half my days, in this dark world and wide,
   And that one talent which is death to hide
   Lodged with me useless, though my soul more bent
To serve therewith my Maker, and present
   My true account, lest he returning chide,
   'Doth God exact day-labour, light denied?'
   I fondly ask. But Patience, to prevent
That murmur, soon replies: 'God doth not need
   Either man's work or his own gifts; who best
   Bear his mild yoke, they serve him best. His state
Is kingly: thousands at his bidding speed,
   And post o'er land and ocean without rest;
   They also serve who only stand and wait.'

SAMUEL BUTLER

(1613–1680)

Born half a century after Shakespeare and Drayton, Butler also came from the English Midlands – Worcestershire. His patron was the notorious dramatist and amorist, George Villiers, 2nd Duke of Buckingham.

Pensioned by Charles II, he still complained of poverty. He wrote a coarse satiric poem of unparalleled popularity – Hudibras. The poem contains many phrases that have since become proverbial, though few people who use them know that they come from Hudibras, or indeed that such a poem exists; among them, 'what's what', 'the main chance', 'to make the mouth water', 'make the fur fly', 'smell a rat'.

from: *Hudibras*

A long satire on the Parliamentarians and Puritans in the Civil War, the ludicrous knight Sir Hudibras and his more effective squire Ralpho being a parody of Don Quixote. The poem was too downmarket for Dr Johnson's taste, who spoke of its (intentionally) 'common thoughts in careless versification' and quoted at Butler the Latin tag: 'Pauper videri Cinna vult, & est pauper' – *'Cinna wishes to seem poor, and is poor.'*

PART I CANTO ONE

The True Blue Presbyterian.

> For his religion it was fit
> To match his learning and his wit:
> 'Twas Presbyterian true Blue,
> For he was of that stubborn crew
> Of errant Saints, whom all men grant
> To be the true Church Militant:
> Such as do build their faith upon
> The holy text of pike and gun;
> Decide all controversies by
> Infallible artillery;
> And prove their doctrine orthodox
> By apostolic blows and knocks;
> Call fire, and sword, and desolation,
> A godly thorough Reformation,
> Which always must be carried on,
> And still be doing, never done:
> As if religion were intended
> For nothing else but to be mended.

Vicarious Punishment among the Saints of New England.

> That Sinners may supply the Place
> Of suff'ring Saints, is a plain case.
> Justice gives sentence many times,
> On one man for another's crimes.
> Our brethren of New England use
> Choice malefactors to excuse,
> And hang the guiltless in their stead,
> Of whom the churches have less need:
> As lately happen'd: in a town
> There lived a cobbler, and but one,
> That out of doctrine could cut use,
> And mend men's lives as well as shoes.
> This precious brother having slain
> In times of peace, an Indian,
> (Not out of malice, but mere zeal,
> Because he was an infidel)

An Indian envoy is sent to the Elders to demand the cobbler's death.

> But they maturely having weighed,
> They had no more but him o' the trade,
> (A man that served them in a double
> Capacity, to teach and cobble)
> Resolved to spare him; yet to do
> The Indian Hoghan Moghan too
> Impartial justice, in his stead did
> Hang an old weaver that was bed-rid.

Women ('the sex') in Marriage – their obsession with Precedence.

> Nor does the Genial Bed provide
> Less for the interests of the Bride: ...
> All women would be of one piece,
> The virtuous matron and the miss;

The nymph of chaste Diana's train,
The same with those in Lewknor's Lane,
But for the difference marriage makes
'Twixt wives and *Ladies of the Lakes:*
Besides the joys of place and birth,
The sex's Paradise on earth;
A privilege so sacred held,
That none will to their mothers yield;
But rather than not go before,
Abandon Heaven at the door.

JOHN DENHAM

(1615–1669)

*Born in Dublin (his maternal grandfather was Lord Drogheda),
Denham was educated at Oxford. A royalist in the Civil Wars, he was
captured, released, and in turn obtained the release of George Wither
the rebel poet. He explained that while Wither lived, Denham 'should
not be the worst poet in England'. At the Restoration he became Surveyor
of Works, his deputy being Christopher Wren. Sir John married his
second wife in Westminster Abbey; she was the Duke of York's mistress.
Denham was yet another 'father of English poetry'. His balanced, anti-
thetical rhyming couplets established a form now most usually associated
with Pope, Dryden and the great Augustans.*

from: *Cooper's Hill*

*This extraordinarily popular poem, about the Egham estate above
Runnymede that Denham inherited, was called by Dr Johnson 'local
poetry'.*

My eye descending from the Hill, surveys
Where *Thames* amongst the wanton valleys strays.

Thames, the most loved of all the Ocean's sons,
By his old Sire to his embraces runs,
Hasting to pay his tribute to the Sea,
Like mortal life to meet Eternity. . . .
O could I flow like thee, and make thy stream
My great example, as it is my theme!
Though deep, yet clear, though gentle, yet not dull,
Strong without rage, without o'er-flowing full. . . .
The stream is so transparent, pure, and clear,
That had the self-enamoured youth[1] gazed here,
So fatally deceived he had not been,
While he the bottom, not his face had seen.

from: *To Sir Richard Fanshaw*
UPON HIS TRANSLATION OF PASTOR FIDO

Fanshaw's translation was of Guarini's Faithful Shepherd. *Denham's
assessment of the translator's art was much praised.*

Such is our pride, our folly, or our fate,
That few but such as cannot write, translate.
But what in them is want of art, or voice,
In thee is either modesty or choice. . . .
That servile path thou nobly dost decline
Of tracing word by word, and line by line.
Those are the laboured births of slavish brains,
Not the effects of Poetry, but pains;
Cheap vulgar arts, whose narrowness affords
No flight for thoughts, but poorly sticks at words.
A new and nobler way thou dost pursue
To make Translations and Translators too.
They but preserve the ashes, thou the flame,
True to his sense, but truer to his fame.

[1] Narcissus.

(1618–1667)

Cowley was a clever London boy who won scholarships to Westminster and Cambridge. The Civil War, in which he was a royalist, caused him to follow the King to Oxford and Henrietta Maria to France. He was arrested briefly as a spy on his return. His interests seem to have been in the country rather than the city. Unlike his friend Thomas Hobbes, author of the Leviathan, *Cowley believed that life could be solitary, moderately poor, and short (like his own), without being 'nasty' or 'brutish'.*

Drinking

The thirsty earth soaks up the rain,
And drinks, and gapes for drink again.
The plants suck in the earth, and are,
With constant drinking, fresh and fair.
The sea itself, which, one would think
Should have but little need of drink,
Drinks twice ten thousand rivers up,
So fill'd, that they o'erflow the cup.
The busy sun, (and one would guess,
By's drunken fiery face, no less,)
Drinks up the sea; and when he's done,
The moon and stars drink up the sun.
They drink and dance by their own light,
They drink and revel all the night.
Nothing in nature's sober found,
But an eternal health goes round.
Fill up the bowl then, fill it high,
Fill all the glasses there: for why
Should every creature drink, but I?
Why, man of morals, tell me why?

JOHN DRYDEN

(1631–1700)

Born into a Puritan family, Dryden was educated at Westminster and Cambridge, wrote a eulogy of Oliver Cromwell, went on to enjoy royal patronage and ended, in James II's reign, by becoming a Roman Catholic. Yet he was no Vicar of Bray, for his conversion ruined him materially. With him we reach another 'father' of English literature: according to Dr Johnson, 'the father of criticism'. It was Dryden who put Shakespeare back on the map, calling the small fry 'little zanies'. Beside criticism, he wrote verse dramas, translations, political satires, odes, and became poet laureate in 1668.

from: *Annus Mirabilis*

The Great Fire of London, 1666, attacks St Paul's.

> Nor could thy fabric, Paul's, defend thee long
>   Tho' thou wert sacred to thy Maker's praise;
> The daring flames peeped in, and saw from far
>   The awful beauties of the sacred choir;
> But since it was profaned by civil war,
>   Heaven thought it fit to have it purged by fire.

Time passes and London is rebuilt.

> More great than human, now, and more august,
>   New deified she from her fires does rise;
> Her widening streets on new foundations trust,
>   And, opening, into larger parts she flies. . . .

> The venturous merchant, who designed more far,
>   And touches on our hospitable shore,
> Charmed with the splendour of this northern star,
>   Shall here unlade him, and depart no more.

from: *Marriage-à-la-Mode*
SONG

Why should a foolish marriage vow,
   Which long ago was made,
Oblige us to each other now
   When passion is decayed?
We loved, and we loved, as long as we could,
   Till our love was loved out in us both;
But our marriage is dead when the pleasure is fled:
   'Twas pleasure first made it an oath.

from: *Song for St Cecilia's Day, 1687*

From harmony, from heavenly harmony
   This universal frame began:
When Nature underneath a heap
      Of jarring atoms lay,
   And could not heave her head,
The tuneful voice was heard from high:
   'Arise, ye more than dead.'
Then cold, and hot, and moist, and dry,
In order to their stations leap,
   And Music's power obey.
From Harmony, from heavenly harmony
   This universal frame began:
   From harmony to harmony
Through all the compass of the notes it ran,
The diapason closing full in Man.

from: *Alexander's Feast*
IN HONOUR OF ST CECILIA'S DAY, 1697

'Twas at the royal feast, for Persia won
   By Philip's warlike son:

Aloft in awful state
The godlike hero sate
    On his imperial throne;
His valiant peers were placed around;
Their brows with roses and with myrtles bound:
    (So should desert in arms be crowned.)
The lovely Thais, by his side,
Sate like a blooming Eastern bride
In flower of youth and beauty's pride.
        Happy, happy, happy pair!
        None but the brave,
        None but the brave,
        None but the brave deserves the fair.

THOMAS SHADWELL

(1642–1692)

*Born in Norfolk, Shadwell succeeded Dryden as poet laureate at the
'Glorious Revolution', which deprived the Catholic Dryden of the
honour. Shadwell might not have acquired his fame but for his quarrel
with the master. Dryden had satirised him as* MacFlecknoe ... the
True-Blew-Protestant Poet T. S. *The reign of James II (also a
Catholic) was more favourable to Dryden's plays than Shadwell's. Then
the situation was reversed. As a sharp, crude critic of Restoration
manners and mores, Shadwell was at his best. He may have died from
an overdose of opium.*

from: *Epsom-Wells*

ACT I SCENE ONE

*A watering-place where ladies of the town and debauchees assemble in
the mornings to wash away their various hangovers. Bains, Bevil and
Woodly are men of 'wit and pleasure'.*

Enter Bains and Bevil.

BEVIL Jack, how is't this morning? We are late, the company is going from the Wells; how does thy last night's work agree with thee?

BAINS Whether that agrees with me or no, I am resolved to agree with that; for no distemper can trouble me that comes from so generous a cause as lusty burgundy and good company.

BEVIL Thou art i' the right, we should no more be troubled at the fevers we get in drinking, than the honourable wounds we receive in battle.

BAINS 'Tis true, the first are the effects of our pleasure, and the last of our honour; which are two things absolutely necessary to the life of a gentleman.

BEVIL Yet your dull splenetic sober sots will tell you we shorten our lives and bring gouts, dropsies, palsies, and the devil and all upon us.

BAINS Let 'em lie and preach on, while we live more in a week than those insipid-temperate fools do in a year. . . . I confess, a disorder got by wine in scurvy company would trouble a man as much as a clap got of a bawd; but there are some women so beautiful, that the pleasure would more than balance the disaster.

BEVIL And as your honest whore-master makes haste to his cure only to be at it again; so do we take pills and the waters to prepare us for another heat.

BAINS For my part I hate to hoard up a great stock of health, as misers do gold, and make no use on't: I am resolved to lay it out upon my friends as far as 'twill go; and if I run myself out, I'll be a good husband for a while to lay it out again when I have it.

BEVIL But, Jack, there are duties to our she, as well as he-neighbours, which the dull, grave, and wise say is lighting our candle at both ends.

BAINS Let 'em light at both ends. Is it not better to let life go out in a blaze than a snuff?

BEVIL I see thou art a brave fellow, and not to be moved by the formal fops of this world.

BAINS I will converse with grave fellows in their books; but with such as thou art over a bottle, Ned. But where's Woodly this morning? I warrant he was drunk last night, and has had a tedious lecture from his impertinent wife; who impudently rails at him, as she says, because she loves him.

BEVIL He's an honest fellow, and ventures hard when he drinks with us; for to say truth, she's a damned wife, but a very good mistress.

BAINS Art not thou a villain to cuckold this honest fellow, and thy friend, Ned?

BEVIL Gad, it's impossible to be a man of honour in these cases. But my intrigue with her began before my friendship with him, so I made a friend of my cuckold, and not a cuckold of my friend.

BAINS An admirable school distinction.

Act V ends with a fake marriage and a divorce celebrated by dance and song.

WOODLY To show you that there was never yet so decent a divorce, I have fiddles to play at it, as they use to do at weddings.

MRS WOODLY And to show you I am extremely pleased, I'll dance at it.

WOODLY How easy and how light I walk without this yoke! methinks 'tis air I tread – Come let's dance, strike up.

DANCE

Marriage that does the hearts and wills unite,
Is the best state of pleasure and delight:
But –
When man and wife no more each other please,
They may at least like us each other ease.

[*Exeunt omnes.*]

MATTHEW PRIOR

(1664–1721)

Son of a Dorset joiner, Prior was educated by his uncle, a vintner, at Westminster School. After Cambridge he rose to become a courtier, ambassador, secretary of state – and elegant satirical poet. When his Tory friends fell from power he was committed for a year to prison for having been a secret agent. He suffered some penury but died on the estate of his friend Lord Oxford. Dr Johnson tells a story of Prior's wit as ambassador at the opera. A Frenchman sitting next to him, in his rapture, accompanied with his own voice the principal singer; whereupon Prior began to rail at the star. The Frenchman defended the star as the stage's chief ornament. 'I know all that,' says the ambassador, 'but he sings so loud I can't hear you.' Prior's epigrams and short pieces are particularly successful.

Epigram

Yes, every poet is a fool;
    By demonstration Ned can show it:
Happy, could Ned's inverted rule
    Prove every fool to be a poet.

A Reasonable Affliction

On his death-bed poor Lubin lies;
    His spouse is in despair;
With frequent sobs, and mutual cries,
    They both express their care.

A different cause, says Parson Sly,
    The same effect may give;
Poor Lubin fears that he shall die;
    His wife, that he may live.

The Remedy Worse than the Disease

I sent for Ratcliffe; was so ill,
 That other doctors gave me over:
He felt my pulse, prescrib'd his pill,
 And I was likely to recover.

But when the wit began to wheeze,
 And wine had warm'd the politician,
Cur'd yesterday of my disease,
 I died last night of my physician.

Epitaph

Nobles and heralds, by your leave,
 Here lies what once was Matthew Prior;
The son of Adam and of Eve,
 Can Bourbon or Nassau go higher?

ROBERT STAPYLTON

(Died 1669)

A Yorkshireman and a monk of Douay in France, Stapylton (or Stapleton) soon found his 'gay and poetical' temperament unsuited to the cloister. He returned to England and became a Protestant. Like Denham, who died in the same year, Stapylton supported the royalist cause, was knighted in 1642 and received a court post at the Restoration. Though he wrote popular verse dramas, of which The Slighted Maid *was seen by Samuel Pepys, his name would probably not be remembered were he not buried in Poets' Corner.*

from: *The Step-Mother*

A TRAGI-COMEDY ACTED WITH GREAT APPLAUSE
AT THE THEATRE IN LITTLE LINCOLN'S-INN-FIELDS
BY THE DUKE OF YORK'S SERVANTS – 1663

*This melodrama about the 'Ancient Britons' in Verulam is full of
marching armies, duels, pretence corpses, fake bards and witches, death-
threats, rape-threats and scaffolds. But this is part comedy; so the wicked
step-mother, Pontia, repents. The 'great Applause' of the audience must
have been due to the play's pace or the popular actors, Mr and Mrs
Betterton. There is some spirited dialogue.*

ACTUS PRIMUS

Pontia's daughter by her first husband, questions Pontia's schemes.

CAESARINA   But Madam, is this Justice?
PONTIA   Give me Power,
      Let honest men, that go to law have Justice:
      Subjects may plead their Titles; Princes must
      Dispute what's Advantageous, not what's Just:
      A Crown he merits, who piles Tower on Tower
      To scale the Stars, and rifle Sovereign Power:
      But he that puts himself into a fright
      With empty sounds, mere terms of Wrong and
      Right,
      Is fitter (when his Conscience checks at them)
      To wear a Mitre than a Diadem.

ACTUS QUINTUS

Filamor and Violinda are to be executed by their step-mother.

FILAMOR   Forgive me, Sister; for thy tender Youth
      My heart bleeds, through my eyes.   [*Weeps.*]
VIOLINDA   Do not afflict
      Yourself for me; the World is full of Ladies,
      And I shall not be missed in that great crowd.

JOSEPH ADDISON

(1672–1719)

One of the many literary sons of clergymen, Addison was educated at Oxford and at thirty-six entered Parliament as a Whig. The following year he contributed to his friend Steele's Tatler, *and with Steele was co-founder of the* Spectator. *Together they were judges of the proprieties of ordinary life. Addison castigated the excesses of Restoration literature. His play* Cato *pleased both Whigs and Tories. He resigned from office in 1718, retiring on a pension. Not till forty-four did he marry: the dowager Countess of Warwick, whose son he tutored. Pope was his rival; fellow writer Thomas Tickell lauded Addison's virtuous life and Christian death:*

> He taught us how to live; and oh! too high
> The price of knowledge, taught us how to die.

from: *Spectator No.26*

ON WESTMINSTER ABBEY, THIS GREAT MAGAZINE OF MORTALITY

When I am in a serious Humour, I very often walk by myself in *Westminster* Abbey; where the Solemnity of the Building, and the Condition of the People who lie in it, are apt to fill the Mind with a kind of Melancholy, or rather Thoughtfulness, that is not disagreeable. . . .

For my own part, though I am always serious, I do not know what it is to be melancholy: and can therefore take a View of Nature in her deep and solemn Scenes, with the same Pleasure as in her most gay and delightful ones. By this means I can improve myself with those Objects, which others consider with Terror. When I look upon the Tombs of the Great, every emotion of Envy dies in me; when I read the Epitaphs of the Beautiful, every inordinate Desire goes out; when I meet with the Grief of Parents upon a Tomb-stone, my Heart melts with Compassion;

when I see the Tomb of the Parents themselves, I consider the Vanity of grieving for those whom we must quickly follow; When I see Kings lying by those who deposed them, when I consider rival Wits placed side by side, or the holy Men that divided the World with their Contests and Disputes, I reflect with Sorrow and Astonishment on the little Competitions, Factions, and Debates of Mankind. When I read the several Dates of the Tombs of some that died Yesterday, and some six hundred Years ago, I consider that great Day when we shall all of us be Contemporaries, and make our Appearance together.

NICHOLAS ROWE

(1674–1718)

Eight poetic dramas and many verse translations fell from Rowe's suave pen; but had not George I created him poet laureate he might not have received burial in Westminster Abbey. Born in Bedfordshire into a prosperous Whig family, Rowe decided to relinquish the law for authorship after his father's death in 1692. Dr Johnson considered his The Fair Penitent *'one of the most pleasing tragedies on the stage, both as to "fable" and "language"', and indeed the glorious Mrs Siddons played the lead in it at Drury Lane. Some contemporary critics considered Rowe to suffer from 'levity of heart' – though in that case it is odd that he failed in his one attempt to write a comedy.*

from: *The Fair Penitent*
PROLOGUE

The poet's plea to write for ordinary people about things as they are.

> Long has the fate of Kings and Empires been
> The common bus'ness of the Tragic Scene,
> As if Misfortune made the Throne her seat,
> And none could be unhappy but the great.

Dearly, 'tis true, each buys the crown he wears,
And many are the mighty Monarch's cares:
By foreign foes and home-bred factions prest,
Few are the joys, and short his hours of rest.
Stories like these with wonder we may hear;
But far remote, and in a higher sphere,
We ne'er can pity what we ne'er can share:
Like distant battles of the Pole and Swede,
Which frugal Citizens o'er coffee read,
Careless for who shall fail or who succeed.

Therefore an humbler theme our author chose,
A melancholy tale of private woes:
No Princes here shall Royalty bemoan,
But you shall meet with sorrows like your own;
Here see imperious Love his vassals treat,
As hardly as ambition does the great;
See how succeeding passions rage by turns,
How fierce the youth with joy and rapture burns,
And how to Death, for beauty lost, he mourns.

Let no nice taste the Poet's art arraign,
If some frail vicious characters he feign:
Who writes should still let Nature be his care,
Mix shades with lights, and not paint all things fair,
But shew you men and women as they are.

JOHN PHILIPS

(1676–1709)

Born in the parsonage of Bampton, Oxfordshire, Philips traced his forebears from the Herefordshire cider country. A scholar of Winchester, he was delicate and popular, loving to have his long hair combed by a friend while he himself read Milton. His name became linked with

Milton's for he wrote in Miltonic blank verse, not the usual rhymed couplets. When he published his famous poem, Cyder, *comparisons between his 'innocuous' apple and Milton's 'forbidden fruit' were inevitable. An admirer wrote:*

> PHILIPS ... who apples sung
> Innocuous, and with freedom bade us quaff
> Their generous nectar ...
> Like Milton too, you taught Britannia's song
> To shake the shackles off of tinkling rhyme.

Philips died of consumption and is buried in Hereford Cathedral.

from: *Cyder*
BOOK I

Choosing the soil for apple trees. This detailed, affectionate account of cider culture helped to inspire Thomson's Seasons. *In the 'Autumn' section he praised Philips, who dared 'With British freedom sing the British song' – cider, of course, being British while the grape was Italian or French.*

> Next, let the planter with discretion meet
> The force and genius of each soil explore,
> To what adapted, what it shuns averse: ...
> The miry fields,
> Rejoicing in rich mould, most ample fruit
> Of beauteous form produce, pleasing to sight,
> But to the tongue inelegant and flat ...
> Nor from the sable ground expect success,
> Nor from cretaceous, stubborn and jejune;
> The must of pallid hue declares the soil
> Devoid of spirit: wretched he that quaffs
> Such wheyish liquors! Oft with colic pangs,
> With pungent colic pangs, distress'd he'll roar,
> And toss, and turn, and curse the unwholesome draught.

But, farmer, look where full-ear'd sheaves of rye
Grow wavy on the tilth; that soil select
For Apples.

Dealing with wasps.

Let every bough
Bear frequent vials, pregnant with the dregs
Of moyle or mum,[1] or treacle's viscous juice;
They by the alluring odour drawn, in haste
Fly to the dulcet cates,[2] and crowding sip
Their palatable bane. Joyful thou'lt see
The clammy surface all o'erstrown with tribes
Of greedy insects, that with fruitless toil
Flap filmy pennons oft to extricate
Their feet, in liquid shackles bound, till death
Bereave them of their worthless souls.

BOOK II

The ideal summer drink.

When dusty summer bakes the crumbling clods
How pleasant is't beneath the twisted arch
Of a retreating bower in mid-day's reign,
To ply the sweet carouse, remote from noise,
Secur'd of feverish heats!

Time to stop.

Therefore, when thy heart
Dilates with fervent joys, and eager soul
Prompts to pursue the sparkling glass, be sure
'Tis time to shun it: if thou wilt prolong
Dire compotation, forthwith reason quits
Her empire to confusion and misrule,

[1] Honey or beer.
[2] Delicacies.

—{ 76 }—

And vain debates; then twenty tongues at once
Conspire in senseless jargon; nought is heard
But din, and various clamour, and mad rant:
Distrust and jealousy to these succeed.
And anger-kindling taunt, the certain bane
Of well-knit fellowship. Now horrid frays
Commence; the brimming glasses now are hurl'd
With dire intent; bottles with bottles clash
In rude encounter; round their temples fly
The sharp-edg'd fragments, down their batter'd cheeks
Mixt gore and Cyder flow.

JOHN GAY

(1685–1732)

*Born in Barnstaple, Devon, Gay was orphaned at ten and apprenticed
to a London silk merchant. He soon returned home, to devote himself
to literature. Though dependent on patronage, he always made some
money from his writings, while* The Beggar's Opera, *with its sequel,*
Polly, *made him famous. He offered* The Beggar's Opera *to John
Rich of the Lincoln's Inn Fields theatre in 1728 and it ran for the then
amazing spell of over sixty days, making 'Gay rich and Rich gay', as
the wits said. There was novelty in its English, Irish and Scottish tunes
instead of the usual Italian, and the subject also was new – 'thieves and
whores'. Jonathan Swift had earlier suggested it to Gay. 'A Newgate
pastoral might make an odd, pretty sort of thing.'*

from: *The Beggar's Opera*
ACT II AIR SEVENTEEN

MACHEATH

How happy could I be with either,
    Were t'other dear charmer away;
But while you thus teaze me together,
    To neither a word will I say;
        But toll de rol, etc.

—{ 77 }—

MAC   Were I laid on Greenland's coast
And in my arms embraced my lass,
Warm amidst eternal frost,
Too soon the half year's night would pass.

POLLY   Were I sold on Indian soil,
Soon as the burning day was closed,
I could mock the sultry toil,
When on my charmer's breast reposed.

MAC   I would love you all the day,

POLLY   Every night would kiss and play;

MAC   If with me you'd fondly stray
Over the hills and far away.

My Own Epitaph

Actually used on his memorial in Poets' Corner.

Life is a jest, and all things show it;
I thought so once and now I know it.

JAMES THOMSON

(1700–1748)

Son of a Scottish pastor, Thomson began writing poetry young – and would burn all his previous compositions on every New Year's Day. He moved from Edinburgh to London as being the only stage for an aspiring poet. His poem 'Winter' was the first to gain him patronage; this was followed by 'Summer', 'Spring' and 'Autumn', the whole eventually making up his popular The Seasons, *an example of genuine nature poetry. During the same period appeared his then famous, now notorious,*

*'Rule Britannia'. His first attempt at tragedy (not his forte) produced
the line:*

O, Sophonisba, Sophonisba, O!

which was parodied as:

O, Jemmy Thomson, Jemmy Thomson, O!

from: *Spring*

On the child in a young family.

By degrees,
The human blossom blows; and every day,
Soft as it rolls along, shows some new charm –
The father's lustre and the mother's bloom.
The infant reason grows, and calls
For the kind hand of an assiduous care.
Delightful task! To rear the tender thought,
To teach the young idea how to shoot.

The Incomparable Soporific Doctor

Dr Patrick Murdoch, a minister.

Sweet, sleeky Doctor! dear pacific soul!
Lay at the beef, and suck the vital bowl!
Still let the involving smoke around thee fly,
And broad-looked dullness settle in thine eye.
Ah! soft in down these dainty limbs repose,
And in the very lap of slumber doze;
But chiefly on the lazy day of grace,
Call forth the lambent glories of thy face;
If aught the thoughts of dinner can prevail –
And sure the Sunday's dinner cannot fail.
To the thin church in sleepy pomp proceed,
And lean on the lethargic book thy head.

These eyes wipe often with the hallowed lawn
Profoundly nod, immeasurably yawn.
Slow let the prayers by thy meek lips be sung,
Nor let thy thoughts be distanced by thy tongue;
If ere the lingerers are within a call,
Or if on prayers thou deign'st to think at all.
Yet – only yet – the swimming head we bend;
But when serene, the pulpit you ascend,
Through every joint a gentle horror creeps,
And round you the consenting audience sleeps.
So when an ass with sluggish front appears,
The horses start, and prick their quivering ears;
But soon as ere the sage is heard to bray,
The fields all thunder, and they bound away.

from: *Rule Britannia*

When Britain first, at Heaven's command,
    Arose from out the azure main,
This was the charter of the land,
    And guardian angels sung this strain.
    'Rule, Britannia, rule the waves,
    Britons never will be slaves.'

The nations, not so blest as thee,
    Must, in their turns, to tyrants fall;
While thou shalt flourish great and free,
    The dread and envy of them all.
    'Rule,' &c. ...

The Muses, still with freedom found,
    Shall to thy happy coast repair:
Blest isle! with matchless beauty crowned,
    And manly hearts to guard the fair:
    'Rule, Britannia, rule the waves,
    Britons never will be slaves.'

SAMUEL JOHNSON

(1709–1784)

Dr Johnson's brilliant and often highly critical Lives of the Poets *tends to conceal the fact that he became a poet himself; though far more illustrious as lexicographer and epigrammatist. Born in Lichfield, he was subject to too many turns of melancholy and ill health to make a successful provincial schoolmaster, as he attempted. With his best pupil, the actor Garrick, he sought and found his fortune in London. 'When a man is tired of London,' his friend James Boswell was later to report Johnson as saying, 'he is tired of life.' He became a bereft widower at forty-three. Women were important to him, as was the Church and State, represented by the Tories. The Whigs he dismissed as 'a faction'. In a poem* The Scholar's Life, *William Mason, one of Johnson's contemporaries, cited the perils of poverty that scholars always risked. Johnson endured much early poverty as well as ill health. According to Mason, if scholars were honoured it would be only after they were buried:*

> 'nations slowly wise and meanly just,
> To buried merit raise the tardy bust.'

A fine bust by Joseph Nollekens was 'raised' extremely 'tardily' (1959) on the wall above Johnson's grave in Poets' Corner.

from: *London*

IN IMITATION OF THE THIRD SATIRE OF JUVENAL

Dr Johnson regrets the loss of a friend but commends his decision to leave London; incidentally a different city from the London of Boswell's reported epigram above.

> For who would leave, unbrib'd, *Hibernia's* Land
> Or change the Rocks of *Scotland* for the *Strand*?
> There none are swept by sudden Fate away,
> But all whom Hunger spares, with Age decay:

Here Malice, Rapine, Accident, conspire,
And now a Rabble rages, now a Fire;
Their ambush here relentless Ruffians lay,
And here the fell Attorney prowls for Prey;
Here falling Houses thunder on your head,
And here a female Atheist talks you dead.

A Parody of the Contemporary Poet Dr Thomas Percy

I put my hat upon my head
And walk'd into the Strand,
And there I met another man
Whose hat was in his hand.

from: Prologue, Spoken by Mr Garrick at the Opening of the Theatre Royal, Drury Lane, 1747

When Learning's triumph o'r her barb'rous foes
First reared the stage, immortal Shakespeare rose;
Each change of many-colour'd life he drew,
Exhausted worlds, and then imagin'd new:
Existence saw him spurn her bounded reign.
And panting Time toiled after him in vain:
His pow'rful strokes presiding truth impress'd
And unresisted passion storm'd the breast. ...
    The wits of Charles found easier ways to fame,
Nor wish'd for Jonson's art, or Shakespeare's flame;
Themselves they studied, as they felt they writ,
Intrigue was plot, obscenity was wit.
Vice always found a sympathetic friend;
They pleased their age, and did not aim to mend. ...
    But who the coming changes can presage,
And mark the future periods of the stage? ...

Hard is his lot, that here by fortune placed,
Must watch the wild vicissitudes of taste;
With ev'ry meteor of caprice must play,
And chase the new-born bubbles of the day.
Ah! let not censure term our fate our choice,
The stage but echoes back the public voice.
The drama's laws the drama's patrons give,
For we that live to please must please to live.

On Hearing Miss Thrale Deliberate about her Hat

Should she wear a new gown and hat to an assembly?

Wear the gown, and wear the hat,
Snatch thy pleasures while they last;
Hadst thou nine lives like a cat,
Soon those nine lives would be past.

Dr Johnson's sayings on Poetry and Sculpture – as reported by Boswell.

BOSWELL Then, Sir, what is Poetry?
JOHNSON Why Sir, it is much easier to say what it is not. We all *know* what light is; but it is not easy to *tell* what it is.

'. . . a fellow will hack half a year at a block of marble to make something in stone that hardly resembles a man. The value of statuary is owing to its difficulty. You would not value the finest head cut upon a carrot.'

Does that put paid to the poetry and statuary in Poets' Corner?

THOMAS GRAY

(1716–1771)

Son of a London scrivener, Gray was educated at Eton and Cambridge. After travelling with the writer Horace Walpole, he returned to Cambridge which he never again left – though he changed colleges from Peterhouse to Pembroke, since the former's students were 'noisy and rude'. He wrote poetry seriously from the age of 26. Dr Johnson admired his life even more than his poetry. Gray 'had the honour of refusing the laurel [laureateship]', and became Professor of Modern History, 'always designing lectures but never reading [delivering] them' and was 'learned and virtuous in most disciplines'. His friend and fellow poet William Mason named his only faults: 'effeminacy and visible fastidiousness'. Polishing every line as he wrote it, Gray made no rough copies.

from: *Ode on a Distant Prospect of Eton College*

> Say, Father Thames, for thou hast seen
> Full many a sprightly race
> Disporting on thy margent green
> The paths of pleasure trace,
> Who foremost now delight to cleave
> With pliant arm thy glassy wave?[1]
> The captive linnet which enthral?
> What idle progeny succeed
> To chase the rolling circle's speed,
> Or urge the flying ball? . . .
>
> Alas, regardless of their doom,
> The little victims play!
> No sense have they of ills to come,
> Nor care beyond today;
> Yet see how all around 'em wait
> The ministers of human fate,

[1] Oarsmen.

And black Misfortune's baleful train!
Ah, show them where in ambush stand
To seize their prey the murtherous band!
Ah, tell them, they are men! . . .

To each his sufferings: all are men,
Condemned alike to groan:
The tender for another's pain,
The unfeeling for his own.
Yet ah! why should they know their fate?
Since sorrow never comes too late,
And happiness too swiftly flies.
Thought would destroy their paradise.
No more; where ignorance is bliss,
'Tis folly to be wise.

from: *Elegy Written in a Country Churchyard*

The curfew tolls the knell of parting day,
The lowing herd wind slowly o'er the lea,
The ploughman homeward plods his weary way
And leaves the world to darkness and to me. . . .

Beneath those rugged elms, that yew-tree's shade,
Where heaves the turf in many a mouldering heap,
Each in his narrow cell for ever laid,
The rude forefathers of the hamlet sleep. . . .

Let not Ambition mock their useful toil,
Their homely joys and destiny obscure;
Nor Grandeur hear, with a disdainful smile
The short and simple annals of the poor.

The boast of heraldry, the pomp of power,
And all that beauty, all that wealth e'er gave,
Awaits alike the inevitable hour.
The paths of glory lead but to the grave. . . .

Far from the madding crowd's ignoble strife
Their sober wishes never learned to stray;
Along the cool sequestered vale of life
They kept the noiseless tenor of their way.

Yet even these bones from insult to protect
Some frail memorial still erected nigh,
With uncouth rhymes and shapeless sculpture decked,
Implores the passing tribute of a sigh. . . .

For who to dumb Forgetfulness a prey,
This pleasing anxious being e'er resigned,
Left the warm precincts of the cheerful day,
Nor cast one longing lingering look behind?

WILLIAM MASON

(1725–1797)

Mason's chief claim to fame lies not in his own poetry but in his services to Thomas Gray, whose friend, editor and biographer he was, as well as author of a charming epitaph. The fashionable cult of the 'Picturesque' greatly interested Mason. It affected painting and landscape gardening; and the idea of rough, wild Nature, untampered with by man, was to influence the Romantic movement in poetry. Though in its excesses Mason came to mock the 'Picturesque', in his long poem, The English Garden, *he gave it its due.*

from: *The English Garden*, *1771–1781*
BOOK III

The making of ha-has, hedges, fences and walls having been discussed, the poem comes on to shade-giving shrubs.

But if our song
Supply one precept here, it bids retire
Each leaf of deeper dye, and lift in front
Foliage of paler verdure, so to spread
A canvas, which when touch'd by Autumn's hand
Shall gleam with dusky gold, or russet rays.
But why prepare for her funereal hand
That canvas? she but comes to dress thy shades,
As lovelier victims for their wintry tomb.
Rather to flowery Spring, to Summer bright,
Thy labour consecrate; their laughing reign,
The youth, the manhood of the growing year,
Deserves that labour, and rewards its pain.
Yet, heedful ever of that ruthless time
When Winter shakes their stems, preserve a file
With everduring leaf to brave his arm,
And deepening spread their undiminish'd gloom.

from: *Sonnet XI*

OCCASIONED BY A LATE ATTACK ON THE PRESENT TASTE OF ENGLISH GARDENS

Two well-travelled cognoscenti *have been 'prating' of the need for Picturesqueness; Good Taste replies on behalf of the goddess Nature.*

'Let them prate
While to my genuine Votaries I assign
The pleasing task from her too rustic state
To lead the willing Goddess; to refine,
But not transform, her charms, and at her shrine
Bid Use with Elegance obsequious wait.'

Sonnet XII

Smooth, simple Path! whose undulating line,
  With sidelong tufts of flow'ry fragrance crown'd,
'Plain in its neatness',[1] spans my garden ground;
What, though two acres thy brief course confine,
Yet sun and shade, and hill and dale are thine,
  And use with beauty here more surely found,
  Than where, to spread the picturesque around,
Cart ruts and quarry holes their charms combine!
  Here, as thou lead'st my step through lawn or grove,
Liberal though limited, restrain'd though free,
  Fearless of dew, or dirt, or dust, I rove,
And own those comforts, all deriv'd from thee!
  Take then, smooth Path, this tribute of my love,
Thou emblem pure of legal liberty!

Epitaph on Mr Gray – In Westminster Abbey

No more the Grecian Muse unrivall'd reigns,
  To Britain let the nations homage pay;
She felt a Homer's fire in Milton's strains,
  A Pindar's rapture from the lyre of GRAY.

OLIVER GOLDSMITH

(c. 1730–1774)

Born in County Longford, the son of a Church of Ireland clergyman, Goldsmith was physically awkward; but his trim, alert mind was well equipped for both satirical and compassionate poetry. His material situation was always precarious. Though he eventually scraped a degree at

---

[1] Milton.

Trinity College, Dublin, his half-hearted assaults on the professions – divinity, medicine – failed. However, his restless travels around Europe, usually penniless except for the odd coin earned by flute-playing, sharpened his wits and further softened his already tender heart. When he began writing, in London, his talents won the friendship of geniuses like Dr Johnson and Sir Joshua Reynolds. He never lost his brogue, and Garrick's quip that Oliver 'wrote like an angel, but spoke like poor Poll' may have been true – assuming that parrots talked with Irish accents.

from: *The Deserted Village*

On depopulation.

> Ill fares the land, to hastening ills a prey,
> Where wealth accumulates, and men decay;
> Princes and lords may flourish, or may fade;
> A breath can make them, as a breath has made;
> But a bold peasantry, their country's pride,
> When once destroyed, can never be supplied.

Elegy on the Death of a Mad Dog

> Good people all, of every sort,
>   Give ear unto my song;
> And if you find it wond'rous short,
>   It cannot hold you long.
>
> In Islington there was a man,
>   Of whom the world might say,
> That still a godly race he ran,
>   Whene'er he went to pray.
>
> A kind and gentle heart he had,
>   To comfort friends and foes;
> The naked every day he clad,
>   When he put on his clothes.

And in that town a dog was found,
    As many dogs there be,
Both mongrel, puppy, whelp, and hound,
    And curs of low degree.

This dog and man at first were friends;
    But when a pique began,
The dog, to gain some private ends,
    Went mad and bit the man.

Around from all the neighbouring streets
    The wond'ring neighbours ran,
And swore the dog had lost his wits,
    To bite so good a man.

The wound it seem'd both sore and sad
    To every Christian eye;
And while they swore the dog was mad,
    They swore the man would die.

But soon a wonder came to light,
    That show'd the rogues they lied:
The man recover'd of the bite,
    The dog it was that died.

RICHARD CUMBERLAND

(1732–1811)

*Born in the master's lodge at Trinity College, Cambridge, Cumberland
was educated at Westminster and Cambridge. Enjoying the patronage
of Lord Halifax, he wrote immensely popular comedies, but was mocked
by Sheridan in* The Critic *as Sir Fretful Plagiary. Garrick called him
a 'man without a skin', Cumberland retorting that he was assailed by
a 'filthy nest of vipers'. His great-grandfather, Bishop Richard Cumber-*

land once said: 'It is better to wear out than to rust out.' Unfortunately his namesake's works are likely to rust out for lack of present-day interest.

from: *The Passive Husband*
ACT III

A light-hearted study of human foibles, in which Sir Toby Truckle's life and that of his daughter, Matilda, are being made a misery by the machinations of his second wife.
Sir Toby Truckle and Lord Glenandry, his friend:

TRUCKLE You are right, my lord – a booby as I was, a blockheadly ass, to think of marrying again, when I had no more need of a wife than a bear has for a blanket. But she took me in with her temper, which was all milk and roses, whilst I courted her; all smiles and dimples in the days of dalliance, till in the extravagance of my folly I was persuaded that she loved me, and began to think she had discovered graces I was not conscious of possessing.

LORD GLEN Guineas, my good Sir Toby, were the graces she discovered, and the smiles and dimples she displayed were caused by the attractions which you carried, not in your person, but in your pockets.

ACT IV

All has ended happily with the exit of Lady Truckle and the betrothal of Matilda and her lover, Clifton. The play was published during the upheavals of the Napoleonic Wars. The master, Shakespeare himself, was said to have 'held up a mirror to nature'.
The last speech:

CLIFTON What happiness on earth can be so great as the possession of a heart like this?

LORD GLEN Then guard it, Clifton, for in times like these virtue needs every prop that we can give it – The world, broke loose from order, arms against it; the law, scarce equal to the task alone, looks to the Muse for succour; and if she, seduced by fashion, hath this night held up a false and specious mirror, dash it from you and break the charm: for we appeal to Nature, and by her candid verdict stand or fall.

JAMES MACPHERSON

(1736–1796)

Clever son of a Scots farmer, Macpherson became an MP and bought himself a tomb in Poets' Corner – and all because of poetry that was partially a cheat. His so-called 'translations' of the alleged Gaelic poet 'Ossian', son of Fingal, deceived thousands, from the blue-stocking Mrs Montagu to Goethe, from the economist Adam Smith to Napoleon. But Dr Johnson, who knew Macpherson's stamping-ground, the Highlands and Islands, spotted the deception: he saw that Macpherson was the creator not the translator of 'Ossian'. Yet an 1830 edition of the poems still gave Macpherson the benefit of the doubt. Admittedly his interest in Gaelic legends was genuine.

from: *Fingal*
AN ANCIENT EPIC POEM

Duchômar, the 'dark man', has spoken admiringly to the lovely maiden Morna.

'From whence,' the fair-haired maid replied, 'from whence Duchômar, most gloomy of men? Dark are thy brows and terrible! Red are thy rolling eyes! . . . What of the foe, Duchômar?' 'From the hill I return, O Morna, from the hill of the dark-brown hinds. Three have I slain with my bended yew. Three with my long bounding dogs of the chase. Lovely daughter of Cormac, I love thee as my soul: I have slain one stately deer for thee. High was his branchy head.' . . . 'Duchômar!' calm the maid replied, 'I love thee not, thou gloomy man! hard is thy heart of rock; dark is thy terrible brow. But Câthba, young son of Torman, thou art the love of Morna. ... Here the daughter of Cormac waits the coming of Câthba!'

'Long shall Morna wait,' Duchômar said, 'long shall Morna wait for Câthba! Behold this sword unsheathed! Here wanders the blood of Câthba. ... He fell by the stream of Branno! On Croma I will raise his tomb, daughter of blue-shielded Cormac! Turn on Duchômar thine eyes; his arm is strong as a storm.' 'Is the son of Torman fallen?' said the wildly-bursting voice of the maid; 'is he fallen on his echoing hills, the youth with the breast of snow? the first in the chase of hinds! the foe of the strangers of ocean? Thou art dark to me, Duchômar; cruel is thine arm to Morna! Give me that sword, my foe! I loved the wandering blood of Câthba!'

He gave the sword to her tears. She pierced his manly breast! He fell, like the bank of a mountain stream, and stretching forth his hand, he spoke: 'Daughter of blue-shielded Cormac! Thou hast slain me in youth! The sword is cold in my breast! Morna; I feel it cold. Give me to Moina the maid. Duchômar was the dream of her night! She will raise my tomb; the hunter shall raise my fame. But draw the sword from my breast. Morna, the steel is cold!' She came, in all her tears she came; she drew the sword from his breast. He pierced her white side! He spread her fair locks on the ground! Her bursting blood sounds from her side: her white arm is stained with red. Rolling in death she lay. The cave re-echoed to her sighs.

RICHARD BRINSLEY SHERIDAN

(1751–1816)

Sheridan may have inherited his dazzling talents as an orator from his Irish father, an actor-manager. His mother was a successful writer. Sheridan's skills as manager of Drury Lane Theatre fell far short of his genius as playwright. He and the theatre were constantly in grave distress, Drury Lane once being burnt down and Sheridan arrested for debt. His real ambitions were political, and he astonished his friends with his scintillating parliamentary speeches. But he lacked the bottom to become a leading minister. Meanwhile he had written two incomparable comedies, satirising the foibles of high society, The Rivals *and* The School for Scandal. *His friend Lord Byron called the latter 'the best comedy' of his day. Linley Sambourne the* Punch *contributor, Lord Dufferin the Viceroy, and Lord Snowdon, were all descended from Sheridan through his beautiful wife, Elizabeth Linley.*

from: *The School for Scandal*
ACT I SCENE ONE

How scandal-mongering works. Mr Crabtree and Sir Benjamin Back-bite are members of the 'school' or group of gossips, with Lady Sneerwell as its queen.

CRABTREE [*To his scandal-mongering cronies*] Did you ever hear how Miss Piper came to lose her lover and her character last summer at Tunbridge? – Sir Benjamin, you remember it?
SIR BENJAMIN Oh, to be sure! – the most whimsical circumstance.
LADY SNEERWELL How was it, pray?
CRABTREE Why, one evening, at Mrs Ponto's assembly, the conversation happened to turn on the breeding Nova Scotia sheep in this country. Says a young lady in company, I have known instances of it – for Miss Letitia Piper, a first cousin of mine, had a Nova Scotia sheep that produced her twins. – What! cries the Lady Dowager Dundizzy (who you know is as deaf as a post), has Miss Piper had twins? – This mistake, as you may imagine, threw the whole company into a fit of laughter. However, 'twas the next morning everywhere reported, and in a few days believed by the whole town, that Miss Letitia Piper had actually been brought to bed of a fine boy and girl; and in less than a week there were some people who could name the father, and the farmhouse where the babies were put to nurse.
LADY SNEERWELL Strange indeed!

Clearly the queen of the 'school' chooses to believe there is no smoke without fire.

ACT III SCENE THREE

Drinking Song by Sir Harry Bumper.

> Here's to the maiden of bashful fifteen;
> Here's to the widow of fifty;
> Here's to the flaunting extravagant quean,
> And here's to the housewife that's thrifty.

Chorus

> Let the toast pass, –
> Drink to the lass,
> I'll warrant she'll prove an excuse for the glass. . . .

> For let 'em be clumsy, or let 'em be slim,
> Young or ancient, I care not a feather;
> So fill a pint bumper quite up to the brim,
> And let us e'en toast them together.

ACT IV SCENE THREE

From the famous 'Screen scene': Sir Peter Teazle, middle-aged husband of a young wife, thinks he has caught out the hypocritical Joseph Surface hiding 'a little French milliner' behind the screen. But it turns out to be somebody else. Charles Surface is Joseph's scapegrace but attractive brother.

SIR PETER . . . He had a girl with him when I called.
CHARLES SURFACE What! Joseph? you jest.
SIR PETER Hush! – a little French milliner – and the best of the jest is – she's in the room now.
CHARLES The devil she is!

—{ 95 }—

SIR PETER Hush! I tell you! [*Points.*]

CHARLES Behind the screen! 'Slife, let's unveil her!

SIR PETER No, no – he's coming – you shan't, indeed!

CHARLES Oh, egad, we'll have a peep at the little milliner!

SIR PETER Not for the world – Joseph will never forgive me –

CHARLES I'll stand by you –

SIR PETER Odds, here he is – [*Joseph Surface enters just as Charles Surface throws down the screen.*]

CHARLES Lady Teazle, by all that's wonderful!

SIR PETER Lady Teazle, by all that's damnable!

WILLIAM BLAKE

(1757–1827)

The son of a London hosier, Blake was born, appropriately enough, in Carnaby Market; two centuries later, Carnaby Street would be the most famous clothiers' mart in England. Blake's genius early showed itself: he wrote verses and was said to have heard 'voices' in childhood. As an engraver's apprentice, he drew the monuments in Westminster Abbey. Did the voices tell him that one day his own would be there? As an adult he showed all the signs of Christian mysticism: his poetry and painting were layered with symbols; he attacked the eighteenth-century materialists; his contemporaries called him mad – though with a madness that was more interesting than other people's sanity. A loving husband and friend, he could be a witty, rough-tongued foe.

from: SONGS OF EXPERIENCE

The Fly

Little Fly,
Thy summer's play
My thoughtless hand
Has brush'd away.

Am not I
A fly like thee?
Or art not thou
A man like me?

For I dance,
And drink, and sing,
Till some blind hand
Shall brush my wing.

The Tyger

Tyger! Tyger! burning bright
In the forests of the night,
What immortal hand or eye
Could frame thy fearful symmetry?

In what distant deeps or skies
Burnt the fire of thine eyes?
On what wings dare he aspire?
What the hand dare seize the fire?

And what shoulder, and what art,
Could twist the sinews of thy heart?
And when thy heart began to beat,
What dread hand? and what dread feet?

What the hammer? What the chain?
In what furnace was thy brain?
What the anvil? What dread grasp
Dare its deadly terrors clasp?

When the stars threw down their spears,
And water'd heaven with their tears,
Did he smile his work to see?
Did he who made the Lamb make thee?

Tyger! Tyger! burning bright
In the forests of the night,
What immortal hand or eye,
Dare frame thy fearful symmetry?

from: *The Everlasting Gospel*

Against the five senses.

This life's five windows of the soul
Distorts the Heavens from pole to pole,
And leads you to believe a lie
When you see with, not thro', the eye.

from: *Gnomic Verses*

Love to faults is always blind;
Always is to joy inclin'd,
Lawless, wing'd and unconfin'd,
And breaks all chains from every mind.

Deceit to secrecy confin'd,
Lawful, cautious and refin'd;
To anything but interest blind,
And forges fetters for the mind.

from: ON FRIENDS AND FOES

On Cromek, who cheated Blake over his engravings.

A petty sneaking knave I knew –
O! Mr Cr___, how do ye do?

Jerusalem

And did those feet in ancient time
  Walk upon England's mountains green?
And was the holy Lamb of God
  On England's pleasant pastures seen?

And did the Countenance Divine
  Shine forth upon our clouded hills?
And was Jerusalem builded here
  Among these dark Satanic Mills?

Bring me my bow of burning gold!
  Bring me my arrows of desire!
Bring me my spear! O clouds, unfold!
  Bring me my chariot of fire!

I will not cease from mental fight,
  Nor shall my sword sleep in my hand,
Till we have built Jerusalem
  In England's green and pleasant land.

from: *The Holiness of Minute Particulars*

Labour well the Minute Particulars: attend to the Little
  Ones,
And those who are in misery cannot remain so long.

from: *To the Christians*

I give you the end of a golden string;
  Only wind it into a ball,
It will lead you in at Heaven's gate,
  Built in Jerusalem's wall.

ROBERT BURNS

(1759–1796)

Born in Ayrshire, Burns was the son of a struggling Scottish tenant farmer. Hard manual labour – but linked with a good education – was the 'ploughman poet's' early lot. Girls were the only delights that such an 'honest-hearted lad' could expect. The first blow to his pride was the veto of his marriage to Jean Armour; it took place several years – and several children – later, when he was famous. But Jean could not satisfy the 'something' in Burns that was 'above the trodden clod'. He was ambitious, and his genius led him to the work for which he was sublimely fitted: 'rescuing, rehabilitating and recreating Scottish folk song' (D. Daiches). His first Poems, Chiefly in the Scottish Dialect, *he published at twenty-seven, and went on to become 'Caledonia's bard'.*

from: *Song*

> Green grow the rashes – O
> Green grow the rashes – O
> The sweetest hours that e'er I spend
> Are spent among the lasses – O.

from: *To a Mouse*

For which the poverty-stricken Burns feels sympathy.

> Wee, sleeket, cowran, tim'rous beastie,
> O, what a panic's in thy breastie!
> Thou need na start awa sae hasty,
>   Wi' bickering[1] brattle!
> I wad be laith[2] to rin an' chase thee,
>   Wi' murd'ring pattle![3]

---

[1] Scamper.   [2] Loath.   [3] Ploughstaff.

I'm truly sorry Man's dominion
Has broken Nature's social union,
An' justifies that ill opinion,
  Which makes thee startle
At me, thy poor, earth-born companion,
  An' fellow-mortal! . . .

Thou saw the fields laid bare an' wast,
An' weary Winter comin fast,
An' cozie here, beneath the blast,
  Thou thought to dwell,
Till crash! the cruel coulter past
  Out thro' thy cell. . . .

But, Mousie, thou art no thy lane,[1]
In proving foresight may be vain:
The best-laid schemes o' Mice and Men
  Gang aft a-gley,[2]
An' leave us nought but grief an' pain,
  For promis'd joy!

from: *The Banks o' Doon*

Ye banks and braes o' bonnie Doon,
  How can ye bloom sae fresh and fair?
How can ye chant, ye little birds,
  And I sae weary, fu' o' care!

Thou'll break my heart, thou warbling bird,
  That wantons thro' the flowering thorn!
Thou minds me o' departed joys,
  Departed never to return.

[1] Alone. [2] Awry.

from: *Auld Lang Syne*

Should auld acquaintance be forgot,
    And never brought to min'?
Should auld acquaintance be forgot,
    And days o' lang syne?

And for auld lang syne, my jo,
    For auld lang syne,
We'll tak a cup o' kindness yet,
    For auld lang syne.

WILLIAM WORDSWORTH

(1770–1850)

Wordsworth's birth in Cumberland, near the Lake District, was to be the most influential factor in his development as a nature poet who was 'haunted' by mountain and cataract 'like a passion'. Two human friendships were equally significant, one with his sister, Dorothy, the other with the poet Coleridge. Together the two poets were responsible for the Lyrical Ballads. *Who would have believed that the young Wordsworth, sympathetic to the French Revolution's ideals and father of an illegitimate child, could ever turn into a poet laureate? Yet he succeeded Robert Southey in the office; both were accused of being 'lost leaders'. Wordsworth enunciated the poetic doctrine of 'emotion recollected in tranquillity' in the Preface to* The Lyrical Ballads *– thereby risking the presence of too much tranquillity and too little emotion. Nevertheless he was outstanding; greatest of the 'Lake Poets'.*

from: *Lines Composed above Tintern Abbey, 1798*

I have learned
To look on nature, not as in the hour
Of thoughtless youth; but hearing often times
The still, sad music of humanity.

Not harsh, nor grating, tho' of ample power
To chasten and subdue. And I have felt
A presence that disturbs me with the joy
Of elevated thoughts; a sense sublime
Of something far more deeply interfused,
Whose dwelling is the light of setting suns,
And the round ocean and the living air,
And the blue sky, and in the mind of man:
A motion and a spirit, that impels
All thinking things, all objects of all thought,
And rolls through all things.

Lyric

A slumber did my spirit seal;
   I had no human fears;
She seemed a thing that could not feel
   The touch of earthly years.

No motion has she now, no force;
   She neither hears nor sees;
Rolled round in earth's diurnal course,
   With rocks, and stones, and trees.

Sonnet Composed upon Westminster Bridge
3 SEPTEMBER 1802

Earth has not anything to show more fair:
Dull would he be of soul who could pass by
A sight so touching in its majesty:
This city now doth like a garment wear
The beauty of the morning; silent, bare,
Ships, towers, domes, theatres, and temples lie
Open unto the fields, and to the sky;
All bright and glittering in the smokeless air.

Never did sun more beautifully steep
In his first splendour, valley, rock or hill;
Ne'er saw I, never felt, a calm so deep!
The river glideth at his own sweet will:
Dear God! the very houses seem asleep;
And all that mighty heart is lying still!

Sonnet
THE WORLD IS TOO MUCH WITH US

The world is too much with us; late and soon,
Getting and spending, we lay waste our powers;
Little we see in Nature that is ours;
We have given our hearts away, a sordid boon!
This Sea that bares her bosom to the moon;
The winds that will be howling at all hours,
And are up-gathered now like sleeping flowers;
For this, for everything, we are out of tune;
It moves us not. – Great God! I'd rather be
A pagan suckled in a creed outworn;
So might I, standing on this pleasant lea,
Have glimpses that would make me less forlorn;
Have sight of Proteus rising from the sea;
Or hear old Triton blow his wreathèd horn.

WALTER SCOTT

(1771–1832)

*Product of Edinburgh in regard to birth, schooling, university and bar,
Scott moved into authorship: first historical poetry, then historical novels,
of which he became the 'father'. He taught younger writers to study the
countryside and to use original historical sources. He could have added
the poet laureateship to the many tributes to his great popularity, but*

declined. He received a baronetcy in 1820. Through his connection with
a publishing failure he was forced to work night and day to pay off his
creditors, at the cost of his own health.

from: *Marmion*
CANTO VI

Lord Marmion, an imaginary descendant of the Norman family, falls
on Flodden field. Abandoned at his own command by his attendants, he
is succoured by the girl he has injured.

'Must I bid twice? – hence, varlets! fly!
Leave Marmion here alone, – to die.'
   They parted, and alone he lay;
   Clare drew her from the sight away,
Till pain wrung forth a lowly moan,
And half he murmur'd, – 'Is there none,
   Of all my halls have nurst,
Page, squire, or groom, one cup to bring
Of blessed water from the spring,
   To slake my dying thirst!'

O, Woman! in our hours of ease,
Uncertain, coy, and hard to please,
And variable as the shade
By the light quivering aspen made;
When pain and anguish wring the brow,
A ministering angel thou! –
Scarce were the piteous accents said,
When, with the Baron's casque, the maid
   To the nigh streamlet ran:
Forgot were hatred, wrongs, and fears,
The plaintive voice alone she hears,
   Sees but the dying man. ...
The war, that for a space did fail,
Now trebly thundering swell'd the gale,

And – Stanley! was the cry; –
  A light on Marmion's visage spread,
    And fired his glazing eye:
With dying hand above his head,
He shook the fragment of his blade,
    And shouted 'Victory! –
Charge, Chester, charge! On, Stanley, on!'
Were the last words of Marmion.

from: *The Heart of Midlothian*

Madge Wildfire, the poor madwoman who lost her wits after being seduced, explains her next move in terms of Pilgrim's Progress, *which her companion, Jeanie Deans, has not read.*

'I am sure,' she continued, 'I may weel say I am come out of the city of Destruction, for my mother is Mrs Bat's-eyes, that dwells at Deadman's corner; and Frank Levitt, and Tyburn Tam, they may be likened to Mistrust and Guilt, that came galloping up, and struck the poor pilgrim to the ground with a great club, and stole a bag of silver, which was most of his spending money, and so have they done to many, and will do to more. But now we will gang to the Interpreter's house, for I ken a man that will play the Interpreter right weel; for he has eyes lifted up to Heaven, the best of books in his hand, the law of truth written on his lips, and he stands as if he pleaded wi' men – Oh, if I had minded what he had said to me, I had never been the castaway creature that I am! – But it is all over now. – But we'll knock at the gate, and then the keeper will admit Christiana, but Mercy will be left out – and then I'll stand at the door, trembling and crying, and then Christiana – that's you, Jeanie – will intercede for me; and then Mercy – that's me, ye ken, will faint; and then the Interpreter, that's Mr Staunton himself, will come out and take me – that's poor, lost, demented me – by the hand, and give me a pomegranate, and a piece of honeycomb, and a small bottle of spirits, to stay my fainting – and then the good times will come back again, and we'll be the happiest folk you ever saw.'

HENRY FRANCIS CARY

(1772–1844)

Cary is another writer who was buried in Poets' Corner on the strength of one oeuvre: his blank verse translation of Dante. Son of an army Officer, he was brought up in Staffordshire, went to Oxford, entered the Church, and became assistant librarian at the British Museum. His unstable temperament (he was twice deranged by family deaths) prevented him from gaining promotion, but his translation put Dante on the insular English map. Thanks to Coleridge, whom he met accidentally on Littlehampton beach, his Dante was publicised. Coleridge had heard Cary spouting Homer to his son and said, 'Sir, yours is a face I should know. I am Samuel Taylor Coleridge.'

from: *The Purgatory*
CANTO IV

Dante is ascending the steep hill of Purgatory and asks his guide about the climb. In his notes Cary explained that the traveller's path in Purgatory grew less evil because 'in ascending he gets rid of the weight of his sins.'

> 'But if it please thee, I would gladly know,
> How far we have to journey: for the hill
> Mounts higher, than this sight of mine can mount.'
>   He thus to me: 'Such is this steep ascent,
> That it is ever difficult at first,
> But more a man proceeds, less evil grows.
> When pleasant it shall seem to thee, so much
> That upward going shall be easy to thee
> As in a vessel to go down the tide,
> Then of this path thou wilt have reach'd the end.
> There hope to rest thee from thy toil. No more
> I answer, and thus far for certain know.'

SAMUEL TAYLOR COLERIDGE

(1772–1834)

Son of a Devonshire vicar, Coleridge was intended for the Church but his expanding taste for philosophy affected his faith and led him into friendships with the Romantic poets. While walking with Southey in the Quantock Hills, he dreamed of a 'Pantisocratic' commune in New England. This friendship was superseded by an intense relationship with William Wordsworth and his sister, Dorothy. He and Wordsworth published the influential Lyrical Ballads. *Brilliant and unstable, Coleridge depended on opium, an addiction that destroyed his intimacy with the Wordsworth circle. This had included Wordsworth's sister-in-law, with whom Coleridge lived, having left his wife, who was Southey's sister-in-law. Rescued by London friends, he concentrated on literary criticism, dying a radical Christian.*

from: *The Rime of the Ancient Mariner*

The Mariner must expiate his crime of shooting an albatross. Towards the end of his penance, a troop of spirits take over his accursed ship, singing 'an angelic song'.

> It ceased; yet still the sails made on
> A pleasant noise till noon,
> A noise like of a hidden brook
> In the leafy month of June,
> That to the sleeping woods all night
> Singeth a quiet tune.

from: *Kubla Khan*
Or, A Vision in a Dream

A fragment written under the influence both of opium and the 'stream-gushing', cavernous Quantocks.

In Xanadu did Kubla Khan
 A stately pleasure-dome decree:
Where Alph, the sacred river, ran
Through caverns measureless to man
 Down to a sunless sea.
So twice five miles of fertile ground
With walls and towers were girdled round:
And there were gardens bright with sinuous rills,
Where blossomed many an incense-bearing tree;
And here were forests ancient as the hills,
Enfolding sunny spots of greenery.

But oh! that deep romantic chasm which slanted
Down the green hill athwart a cedarn cover!
A savage place! as holy and enchanted
As e'er beneath a waning moon was haunted
By woman wailing for her demon-lover!
And from this chasm, with ceaseless turmoil seething,
As if this earth in fast thick pants were breathing,
A mighty fountain momently was forced;
Amid whose swift half-intermitted burst
Huge fragments vaulted like rebounding hail,
Or chaffy grain beneath the thresher's flail:
And 'mid these dancing rocks at once and ever
It flung up momently the sacred river.
Five miles meandering with a mazy motion
Through wood and dale the sacred river ran,
Then reached the caverns measureless to man,
And sank in tumult to a lifeless ocean:
And 'mid this tumult Kubla heard from far
Ancestral voices prophesying war! ...

 A damsel with a dulcimer
 In a vision once I saw:
 It was an Abyssinian maid,
 And on her dulcimer she played,
 Singing of Mount Abora.

Could I revive within me
Her symphony and song,
To such a deep delight 'twould win me,
That with music loud and long,
I would build that dome in air,
That sunny dome! those caves of ice!
And all who heard should see them there,
And all should cry, Beware! Beware!
His flashing eyes, his floating hair!
Weave a circle round him thrice,
And close your eyes with holy dread,
For he on honey-dew hath fed,
And drunk the milk of Paradise.

ROBERT SOUTHEY

(1774–1843)

Son of a Somerset linen-draper, Southey became one of the famous 'Lake Poets', and also one of their 'lost leaders', Wordsworth being another (see Browning's poem). In other words, Southey began as a youthful revolutionary, expelled from Westminster for denouncing flogging in The Flagellant, *a school magazine. He went on to plan with the poet Coleridge (but not to create) a Utopian commune in America which they called 'Pantisocracy'. He and Coleridge married sisters. The first poem quoted below shows the idealist's scepticism about war and victory. But the years brought him 'wisdom': the laureateship, a government pension, enthusiasm for his visit to Waterloo – and verbal skirmishes with a sceptical newcomer, the poet Byron.*

from: *The Battle of Blenheim*

First published in 1798.

It was a summer evening,
   Old Kaspar's work was done,
And he before his cottage door
   Was sitting in the sun,
And by him sported on the green
His little grandchild Wilhelmine.

She saw her brother Peterkin
   Roll something large and round,
Which he beside the rivulet
   In playing there had found,
He came to ask what he had found,
That was so large, and smooth, and round.

Old Kaspar took it from the boy,
   Who stood expectant by;
And then the old man shook his head,
   And, with a natural sigh,
''Tis some poor fellow's skull,' said he,
'Who fell in the great victory.' . . .

'Now tell us what 'twas all about,'
   Young Peterkin, he cries;
And little Wilhelmine looks up
   With wonder-waiting eyes;
'Now tell us all about the war,
And what they fought each other for.'

'It was the English,' Kaspar cried,
   'Who put the French to rout;
But what they fought each other for,
   I could not well make out;
But everybody said,' quoth he,
'That 'twas a famous victory. . . .

'They say it was a shocking sight
   After the field was won;
For many thousand bodies here
   Lay rotting in the sun;
But things like that, you know, must be
After a famous victory. . . .

'And everybody praised the Duke[1]
   Who this great fight did win.'
'But what good came of it at last?'
   Quoth little Peterkin.
'Why, that I cannot tell,' said he,
'But 'twas a famous victory.'

from: *The Poet's Pilgrimage to Waterloo*

Written after 1815. Southey had just visited the Château of Hougou-
mont on the field of Waterloo. Wellington's troops had held it heroically
all day, despite fire and slaughter. Southey's wish that Hougoumont
should be preserved was fulfilled quite recently, thanks to the Anglo-
Belgian Waterloo Committee. His attitude to 'victory' had changed since
1798. It was now genuinely 'great', not ironically 'famous'.

STANZA 55

Thy ruins as they fell should aye remain . . .
   What monument so fit for those below?
Thy garden through whole ages should retain
   The form and fashion which it weareth now,
That future pilgrims here might all things see,
   Such as they were at this great victory.

[1] The Duke of Marlborough.

(1775–1817)

Yet another vicarage-born genius, Miss Austen (as her devotees like to call her – though they call themselves 'Janeites') never married, despite her ability to describe courtships with matchless humour and realism. Her first and last homes were in Hampshire. It is remarkable that the woman who was writing the novel Persuasion *at the time of Waterloo should have allowed scarcely an echo of world affairs to be heard in her stories. She described herself, unconvincingly, as 'the most unlearned, and uninformed female who ever dared to be an authoress'. The historian Macaulay wished he could set up a monument in Winchester Cathedral to 'this wonderful woman'. Today they both have memorials in the Abbey, while Jane has her marble slab in Winchester Cathedral.*

from: *Pride and Prejudice*

The first proposal of Mr Fitzwilliam Darcy, the wealthy, handsome, haughty Norman-blooded hero to Miss Elizabeth Bennet, the pretty, high-spirited heroine.

He sat down for a few moments, and then getting up, walked about the room. Elizabeth was surprised, but said not a word. After a silence of several minutes, he came towards her in an agitated manner, and thus began,

'In vain have I struggled. It will not do. My feelings will not be repressed. You must allow me to tell you how ardently I admire and love you.'

Elizabeth's astonishment was beyond expression. She stared, coloured, doubted, and was silent. This he considered sufficient encouragement, and the avowal of all that he felt and had long felt for her, immediately followed. He spoke well, but there were feelings besides those of the heart to be detailed, and he was not more eloquent on the subject of tenderness than of pride. His sense of her inferiority, of its being a degradation, of the family obstacles which judgment had always opposed to inclination, were dealt on with a warmth which seemed . . . very unlikely to recommend his suit. . . .

He concluded with representing to her the strength of that attachment which in spite of all his endeavours, he had found impossible to conquer; and with expressing his hope that it would now be rewarded by her acceptance of his hand. As he said this she could easily see that he had no doubt of a favourable answer. He *spoke* of apprehension and anxiety, but his countenance expressed real security. Such a circumstance could only exasperate farther; and when he ceased the colour rose into her cheeks and she said,

'In such cases as this, it is, I believe, the established mode to express a sense of obligation for the sentiments avowed, however unequally they may be returned. It is natural that obligation should be felt, and if I could *feel* gratitude, I would now thank you. But I cannot – I have never desired your good opinion, and you have certainly bestowed it most unwillingly.'

There is a pause while the furious Darcy assumes a false calm.

The pause was to Elizabeth's feelings dreadful. At length, in a voice of forced calmness, he said,

'And this is all the reply which I am to have the honour of expecting! I might, perhaps, wish to be informed why, with so little *endeavour* at civility, I am thus rejected. . . .'

'I might as well inquire,' replied she, 'why, with so evident a design of offending and insulting me, you chose to tell me that you liked me against your will, against your reason, and even against your character? Was not this some excuse for incivility, if I *was* uncivil?'

They part in flaming anger; but twenty-six chapters later Darcy's pride and Elizabeth's prejudice have melted in a happy engagement, the result of his kindness to her sisters and family.

Elizabeth's spirits soon rising to playfulness again, she wanted Mr

Darcy to account for his having ever fallen in love with her. 'How could you begin?' said she. 'I can comprehend your going on charmingly when you had once made a beginning; but what could set you off in the first place?'

'I cannot fix on the hour, or the spot, or the look, or the words, which laid the foundation. It is too long ago. I was in the middle before I knew I *had* begun.'

'My beauty you had early withstood, and as for my manners – my behaviour to *you* was at least always bordering on the uncivil . . . Now, be sincere; did you admire me for my impertinence?'

'For the liveliness of your mind I did.'

'You may as well call it impertinence at once. . . . The fact is that you were sick of civility, of deference, of officious attention. You were disgusted with the women who were always speaking and looking, and thinking for *your* approbation alone. I roused, and interested you, because I was so unlike *them*. . . . There – I have saved you the trouble of accounting for it; and really, all things considered, I begin to think it perfectly reasonable. To be sure you know no actual good of me – but nobody thinks of *that* when they fall in love.'

THOMAS CAMPBELL

(1777–1844)

Born in Glasgow, the son of a merchant, Campbell attended Glasgow University and helped found University College, London. His longer poems are forgotten, though there can be few survivors from an older generation who have not, as children, been taught to spout Campbell's patriotic poems, such as 'Ye Mariners of England' (What did 'towers along the steep' mean?), or to weep for Lord Ullin's daughter.

from: *The Pleasure of Hope*

His first published poem.

> At Summer eve, when Heaven's ethereal bow
> Spans with bright arch the glittering hills below,
> Why to yon mountain turns the musing eye,
> Whose sunbright summit mingles with the sky?
> Why do those cliffs of shadowy tint appear
> More sweet than all the landscape smiling near?
> 'Tis distance lends enchantment to the view,
> And robes the mountain in its azure hue.

Song: Men of England

Campbell's Scots blood forbade mere boasting.

> Men of England! who inherit
>   Rights that cost your sires their blood!
> Men whose undegenerate spirit
>   Has been proved on land and flood: –
>
> By the foes ye've fought, uncounted,
>   By the glorious deeds ye've done.
> Trophies captured – breaches mounted,
>   Navies conquered – kingdoms won!
>
> Yet, remember, England gathers
>   Hence but fruitless wreaths of fame,
> If the freedom of your fathers
>   Glow not in your hearts the same.
>
> What are monuments of bravery
>   Where no public virtues bloom?
> What avail in lands of slavery
>   Trophied temples, arch, and tomb?

Pageants! – Let the world revere us
   For our people's rights and laws,
And the breasts of civic heroes
   Bared in Freedom's holy cause.

Yours are Hampden's, Russell's glory,
   Sydney's matchless shade is yours, –
Martyrs in heroic story
   Worth a hundred Agincourts!

We're the sons of sires that baffled
   Crowned and mitred tyranny: –
They defied the field and scaffold
   For their birthrights – so will we!

To a Young Lady
WHO ASKED ME TO WRITE SOMETHING ORIGINAL FOR HER ALBUM

An original something, fair maid, you would win me
To write – but how shall I begin?
For I fear I have nothing original in me –
Excepting Original Sin.

from: *Ode to the Memory of Robert Burns*

After celebrating Burns as a lover, Campbell continues:

Nor skilled one flame alone to fan:
His country's high-souled peasantry
What patriot pride he taught! how much
To weigh the inborn worth of man!
And rustic life and poverty
Grew beautiful beneath his touch.

GEORGE GORDON BYRON

(1788–1824)

Byron was born in London though 'half a Scot' and became 6th Baron in 1798. He was often spoken of as 'Romantic', and indeed his wildly popular lyric verse possessed all the authentic die-away notes of romantic nostalgia. His club foot did nothing to diminish the effect, while his youthful beauty enhanced it. Nevertheless he was man-of-the-worldly rather than dreamily poetic. Byron's mature poetry lashed his contemporaries with satiric wit and his style in Don Juan, *his masterpiece, is brilliantly conversational as well as serious. As an exile from England, after a disastrous marriage and separation owing mainly to his way of life, he formed a 'last attachment' to Countess Guiccioli in Italy, where he sympathised with the country's independence movement. He gave his life in the cause of Greek freedom and is still proudly remembered there. Half jokingly expecting a memorial in Westminster Abbey or St Paul's, he had to wait till 1969 for a stone in Poets' Corner, the pleas of Hardy and Kipling on Byron's behalf having been rejected in 1924.*

So, We'll Go no more A-roving

So, we'll go no more a-roving
    So late into the night,
Though the heart be still as loving,
    And the moon be still as bright.

For the sword outwears its sheath,
    And the soul wears out the breast,
And the heart must pause to breathe,
    And love itself have rest.

Though the night was made for loving,
    And the day returns too soon,
Yet we'll go no more a-roving
    By the light of the moon.

from: *Don Juan*

The isles of Greece, the isles of Greece!
   Where burning Sappho loved and sung,
Where grew the arts of war and peace,
   Where Delos rose, and Phoebus sprung!
Eternal summer gilds them yet,
But all, except their sun, is set. ...

The mountains look on Marathon –
   And Marathon looks on the sea;
And musing there an hour alone,
   I dream'd that Greece might still be free;
For standing on the Persians' grave
I could not deem myself a slave.

CANTO XIV

William Wilberforce was the champion of the anti-slavery cause.

O Wilberforce! thou man of black renown,
   Whose merit none enough can sing or say,
Thou hast struck one immense Colossus down,
   Thou moral Washington of Africa!
But there's another little thing, I own,
   Which you should perpetrate some summer's day,
And set the other half of earth to rights;
You have freed the *blacks* – now pray shut up the whites.

CANTO XV

Between two worlds life hovers like a star,
   'Twixt night and morn, upon the horizon's verge.
How little do we know that which we are!
   How less what we may be! The eternal surge
Of time and tide rolls on, and bears afar
   Our bubbles; as the old burst, new emerge,
Lash'd from the foam of ages; while the graves
Of empires heave but like some passing waves.

The Sword, the Banner, and the Field,
  Glory and Greece around me see!
The Spartan borne upon his shield.
  Was not more free. . . .

If thou regrett'st thy youth, *why live?*
  The land of honourable death
Is here – up to the Field, and give
  Away thy breath!

Seek out – less often sought than found –
  A soldier's grave, for thee the best;
Then look around, and choose thy ground,
  And take thy Rest.

JOHN KEBLE

(1792–1866)

*An 'Oxford man' par excellence, Keble graduated at Oxford, became
Oxford Professor of Poetry and had a powerful creative influence on the
(Anglo-Catholic) Oxford Movement, or Tractarians, so-called because
of their propaganda carried on through their* Tracts for the Times.
Among other writings are his contributions to Hymns Ancient and
Modern, *the Anglican hymnal, and to the hymnals of other Churches.
Not all Keble's hymns are sung equally often since some are relevant to
specialised subjects such as 'Rogation' and 'Theological Colleges'; but his
hymn on 'Holy Matrimony' is surely the most popular piece on the
subject ever written by a celibate.*

from: *Holy Matrimony*

The voice that breathed o'er Eden,
  That earliest wedding day,
The primal marriage blessing,
  It hath not pass'd away:

Still in the pure espousal
   Of Christian man and maid
The Holy Three are with us,
   The threefold grace is said,

For dower of blessed children,
   For love and faith's sweet sake,
For high mysterious union
   Which nought on earth may break. ...

O spread thy pure wing o'er them
   Let no ill power find place,
When onward to Thine Altar
   The hallow'd path they trace.

PERCY BYSSHE SHELLEY

(1792–1822)

If ever anyone seemed born to conventional worldly success, it was Shelley. Son of a wealthy landed Member of Parliament for a constituency in East Sussex, Shelley nevertheless got himself expelled from Oxford for militant atheism, to which he was soon to add free love, republicanism and vegetarianism. Add further a brilliant gift with ideas and words, and you have a dazzling revolutionary comet of the Romantic movement. He eloped twice; his first wife, Harriet Westbrook, drowned herself in the Serpentine, his second wife Mary Godwin, daughter of the radical philosopher, wrote Frankenstein. *Shelley and Byron formed the nucleus of a bohemian literary colony in Pisa. Byron's natural child Allegra, who died aged 5, was befriended by Shelley, though Shelley was not too careful about the health of his own three children, two of whom died on their travels. The Pisa colony lasted until Shelley was drowned in a sailing accident in the Bay of Spezia; he and Byron were to meet again in the 'colony' at Poets' Corner, which they both had difficulty in entering.*

Ozymandias

I met a traveller from an antique land
Who said: Two vast and trunkless legs of stone
Stand in the desert ... Near them, on the sand,
Half sunk, a shattered visage lies, whose frown,
And wrinkled lip, and sneer of cold command,
Tell that its sculptor well those passions read
Which yet survive, stamped on these lifeless things,
The hand that mocked them, and the heart that fed.
And on the pedestal these words appear:
'My name is Ozymandias, king of kings:
Look on my works, ye Mighty, and despair!'
Nothing beside remains. Round the decay
Of that colossal wreck, boundless and bare
The lone and level sands stretch far away.

from: *Prometheus Unbound*
I

Poetic genius.

> On a poet's lips I slept
> Dreaming like a love-adept
> In the sound his breathing kept;
> Nor seeks nor finds he mortal blisses,
> But feeds on the aërial kisses
> Of shapes that haunt thought's wildernesses.
> He will watch from dawn to gloom
> The lake-reflected sun illume
> The yellow bees in the ivy bloom,
> Nor heed, nor see, what things they be;
> But from these create he can
> Forms more real than living man,
> Nurslings of immortality!

from: *To a Skylark*

Human limitations.

We look before and after,
    And pine for what is not:
Our sincerest laughter
    With some pain is fraught;
Our sweetest songs are those that tell of saddest thought.

from: *Ode to the West Wind*

The poet's vocation.

Make me thy lyre, even as the forest is:
    What if my leaves are falling like its own?
The tumult of thy mighty harmonies

    Will take from both a deep autumnal tone,
Sweet though in sadness. Be thou, Spirit fierce,
    My spirit! Be thou me, impetuous one!

Drive my dead thoughts over the universe,
    Like withered leaves, to quicken a new birth;
And, by the incantation of this verse,

    Scatter, as from an unextinguished hearth
Ashes and sparks, my words among mankind!
    Be through my lips to unawakened earth

The trumpet of a prophecy! O wind,
    If Winter comes, can Spring be far behind?

from: *Adonais*

In this elegy on the death of Keats, Shelley might be describing his own coming death by shipwreck.

> The breath whose might I have invoked in song
> Descends on me; my spirit's bark is driven,
> Far from the shore, far from the trembling throng
> Whose sails were never to the tempest given;
> The massy earth and spherèd skies are riven!
> I am borne darkly, fearfully, afar;
> Whilst, burning through the inmost veil of Heaven,
> The soul of Adonais, like a star,
> Beacons from the abode where the Eternal are.

JOHN CLARE

(1793–1864)

Clare's most recent editors have called his poetry 'a miracle' – he was a Northamptonshire agricultural labourer, the son of an illiterate mother and a father who could sing ballads and read bits of the Bible. After the successful publication of his early Rural Life and Scenery, *Clare's popularity and patronage fell away, until in 1908 the editor of the* Dictionary of National Biography *wrote of him: 'his poetry does not rise to a really high level'. Today, however, he is spoken of as a major poet. He spent his last twenty-seven years in the Northampton Lunatic Asylum, from which poems, many of them beautiful, continued to pour.*

Life's Likenesses

> Life is – what?
> It is the shooting of a star,
> That gleams along the trackless air,
> And vanishes, almost ere seen, to nought.

And such is Man –
He shines and flutters for a span,
   And is forgot.

Life is – what?
It is the vermeil of the rose,
That blooms but till the bleak wind blows,
Then, all entomb'd in sweets, doth fade and rot.
And such is Man –
He struts in brav'ry for a span,
   And is forgot.

The Peasant Poet

Written in Northampton Asylum.

He loved the brook's soft sound
The swallow swimming by
He loved the daisy covered ground
The cloud bedappled sky.
To him the dismal storm appeared
The very voice of God,
And where the evening rock was reared
Stood Moses with his rod.

And every thing his eyes surveyed
The insects in the brake
Were creatures God Almighty made
He loved them for his sake.
A silent man in life's affairs
A thinker from a boy
A peasant in his daily cares –
The poet in his joy.

I am

I am: yet what I am none cares or knows,
   My friends forsake me like a memory lost;
I am the self-consumer of my woes,
   They rise and vanish in oblivious host,
Like shades in love and death's oblivion lost;
And yet I am, and live with shadows tost

Into the nothingness of scorn and noise,
   Into the living sea of waking dreams,
Where there is neither sense of life nor joys,
   But the vast shipwreck of my life's esteems;
And e'en the dearest – that I loved the best –
Are strange – nay, rather stranger than the rest.

I long for scenes where man has never trod,
   A place where woman never smiled or wept;
There to abide with my creator, God,
   And sleep as I in childhood sweetly slept:
Untroubling and untroubled where I lie,
The grass below – above the vaulted sky.

JOHN KEATS

(1795–1821)

Described as 'the most loveable creature', Keats was born over a stable in London; his touchingly devoted literary friends regarded him as a star of the 'Romantic movement', though hostile reviewers would substitute 'Cockney' for 'Romantic'. Keats trained as an apothecary but soon dedicated himself wholly to poetry. His fiancée, Fanny Brawne, has been criticised for coldness; but at least she wore mourning for seven years after his death. He died in Rome, in the misery of tuberculosis, choosing for his own tombstone: 'Here lies one whose name was writ in water.'

Yet his inner vision of beauty has made sure that no name should be worthier to be 'writ in' the marble of Poets' Corner.

Sonnet

Written in the fields, June 1816.

To one who has been long in city pent,
　　'Tis very sweet to look upon the fair
　　And open face of heaven, – to breathe a prayer
Full in the smile of the blue firmament.
Who is more happy, when, with heart's content,
　　Fatigued he sinks into some pleasant lair
　　Of wavy grass, and reads a debonair
And gentle tale of love and languishment?
Returning home at evening, with an ear
　　Catching the notes of Philomel, – an eye
Watching the sailing cloudlet's bright career,
　　He mourns that day so soon has glided by:
E'en like the passage of an angel's tear
　　That falls through the clear ether silently.

Ode on a Grecian Urn

Thou still unravish'd bride of quietness,
　　Thou foster-child of silence and slow time,
Sylvan historian, who canst thus express
　　A flowery tale more sweetly than our rhyme:
What leaf-fring'd legend haunts about thy shape
　　Of deities or mortals, or of both,
　　　In Tempe or the dales of Arcady?
What men or gods are these? What maidens loth?
　　What mad pursuit? What struggle to escape?
　　　What pipes and timbrels? What wild ecstasy?

Heard melodies are sweet, but those unheard
   Are sweeter; therefore, ye soft pipes, play on;
Not to the sensual ear, but, more endear'd,
   Pipe to the spirit ditties of no tone:
Fair youth, beneath the trees, thou canst not leave
   Thy song, nor ever can those trees be bare;
     Bold Lover, never, never canst thou kiss,
Though winning near the goal – yet, do not grieve;
   She cannot fade, though thou hast not thy bliss,
     For ever wilt thou love, and she be fair! . . .

Who are these coming to the sacrifice?
   To what green altar, O mysterious priest,
Lead'st thou that heifer lowing at the skies,
   And all her silken flanks with garlands drest?
What little town by river or sea-shore,
   Or mountain-built with peaceful citadel,
     Is emptied of this folk, this pious morn?
And, little town, thy streets for evermore
   Will silent be; and not a soul to tell
     Why thou art desolate, can e'er return.

O Attic shape! Fair attitude! with brede[1]
   Of marble men and maidens overwrought,
With forest branches and the trodden weed;
Thou, silent form, dost tease us out of thought
As doth eternity: Cold Pastoral!
   When old age shall this generation waste,
     Thou shalt remain, in midst of other woe
Than ours, a friend to man, to whom thou say'st,
   'Beauty is truth, truth beauty, – that is all
     Ye know on earth, and all ye need to know.'

[1] Braid, embroidery.

LORD MACAULAY

(1800–1859)

Son of a famous anti-slavery propagandist, Thomas Babington Macaulay, the future Whig peer, was himself a reformer in Parliament and on the India Council. He was also a brilliant historian and essayist whose eloquence sometimes burst into blazing rhetoric. His History of England *was immensely popular, as were his* Lays of Ancient Rome. *The nostalgic celebration in the* Lays *of 'the brave days of old' may seem a curious stance for a forward-looking Whig. But Macaulay was picturing Rome as the centre of civic virtues which he expected soon to see flourishing in enlightened Victorian England.*

from: *The Lays of Ancient Rome*
HORATIUS

The Tuscan hosts are about to invade Rome by the bridge over the River Tiber. Horatius, captain of the gate, and two other volunteers offer to hold back the Tuscans until the bridge has been demolished.

> 'Horatius,' quoth the Consul,
>   'As thou sayest, so let it be,'
> And straight against that great array
>   Forth went the dauntless Three.
> For Romans in Rome's quarrel
>   Spared neither land nor gold,
> Nor son nor wife, nor limb nor life
>   In the brave days of old.
>
> Then none was for a party;
>   Then all were for the state;
> Then the great man helped the poor,
>   And the poor man loved the great;

Then lands were fairly portioned;
    Then spoils were fairly sold;
The Romans were like brothers
    In the brave days of old. ...

*The dauntless three defeat all challengers; but meanwhile the bridge is
about to fall. His comrades dart back; the wounded Horatius prepares
to swim for it.*

'Oh, Tiber! father Tiber!
    To whom the Romans pray.
A Roman's life, a Roman's arms,
    Take thou in charge this day.'
So he spake, and speaking sheathed
    The good sword by his side
And with his harness on his back,
    Plunged headlong in the tide.

No sound of joy or sorrow
    Was heard from either bank;
But friends and foes in dumb surprise,
With parted lips and straining eyes,
    Stood gazing where he sank.
And when above the surges
    They saw his crest appear,
All Rome sent forth a rapturous cry,
And even the ranks of Tuscany
    Could scarce forbear to cheer.

from: ESSAYS AND BIOGRAPHIES

from: *Warren Hastings*

*The last of nearly 150 pages written by Macaulay on G. R. Gleig's
three-volume* Memoirs *of the first Governor-General of Bengal,*
Warren Hastings.

With all his faults, – and they were neither few nor small, – only one cemetery was worthy to contain his remains. In that temple of silence and reconciliation where the enmities of twenty generations lie buried, in the Great Abbey[1] which has during many ages afforded a quiet resting-place to those whose minds and bodies have been shattered by the contentions of the Great Hall,[2] the dust of the illustrious accused should have mingled with the dust of the illustrious accusers. This was not to be. Yet the place of interment was not ill chosen. Behind the chancel of the parish church of Daylesford, in earth which already held the bones of many chiefs of the house of Hastings, was laid the coffin of the greatest man who has ever borne that ancient and widely extended name. . . .

His principles were somewhat lax. His heart was somewhat hard. But though we cannot with truth describe him either as a righteous or as a merciful ruler, we cannot regard without admiration the amplitude and fertility of his intellect, his rare talents for command, for administration, and for controversy, his dauntless courage, his honourable poverty, his fervent zeal for the interests of the state, his noble equanimity, tried by both extremes of fortune, and never disturbed by either.

HENRY WADSWORTH LONGFELLOW

(1807–1882)

Longfellow was born in Maine and became Professor of Modern Languages, first at Bowdoin, Brunswick, then at Harvard. He was twice widowed, the second time when his wife was burnt to death through an accident with lighted sealing wax. Perhaps the most popular poet in the English-speaking world, he was nominated for this honour by W. M. Rossetti, one of his early editors, who put him before even Tennyson, except in England. The reason given was Longfellow's great feeling for 'the spirit of the age'. This 'spirit' included religious devotion, advocacy

---

[1] Westminster.
[2] Westminster Hall where Hastings was tried and acquitted.

of the rights of Blacks (Poems on Slavery, *1842*), *interest in national legend and history* (Hiawatha), *sentimental romance* (Evangeline, 'Excelsior').

The Slave's Dream

Beside the ungathered rice he lay,
  His sickle in his hand;
His breast was bare, his matted hair
  Was buried in the sand.
Again, in the mist and shadow of sleep,
  He saw his Native Land.

Wide through the landscape of his dreams
  The lordly Niger flowed;
Beneath the palm-trees on the plain
  Once more a king he strode;
And heard the tinkling caravans
  Descend the mountain road.

He saw once more his dark-eyed queen
  Among her children stand;
They clasped his neck, they kissed his cheeks,
  They held him by the hand! –
A tear burst from the sleeper's lids
  And fell into the sand.

And then at furious speed he rode
  Along the Niger's bank;
His bridle-reins were golden chains,
  And, with a martial clank,
At each leap he could feel his scabbard of steel
  Smiting his stallion's flank.

Before him, like a blood-red flag,
  The bright flamingoes flew;
From morn till night he followed their flight,
  O'er plains where the tamarind grew,
Till he saw the roofs of Caffre huts,
  And the ocean rose to view.

At night he heard the lion roar,
    And the hyena scream;
And the river-horse, as he crushed the reeds
    Beside some hidden stream;
And it passed, like a glorious roll of drums,
    Through the triumph of his dream.

The forest, with their myriad tongues,
    Shouted of liberty;
And the Blast of the Desert cried aloud,
    With a voice so wild and free,
That he started in his sleep and smiled
    At their tempestuous glee.

He did not feel the driver's whip,
    Nor the burning heat of day;
For death had illumined the Land of Sleep,
    And his lifeless body lay
A worn-out fetter, that the soul
    Had broken and thrown away!

ALFRED, LORD TENNYSON

(1809–1892)

Born in Lincolnshire, Tennyson was a rector's son, yet another poet with a Church background. The landmarks in his early life were friendships and literary success at Cambridge. It was the death of his friend Arthur Hallam that focused, in his poem In Memoriam, *many Victorian views on religion and evolution. Several factors combined in this century to lower Tennyson's reputation from its Victorian summit, when he was honoured as poet laureate: his exaggerated homage to the Prince Consort, causing the poet Swinburne to parody Tennyson's* Morte D'Arthur *as the 'Morte D'Albert'; and the mellifluous richness of his verse at a time when that, like royal adulation, was going out of fashion. His rediscovered temperamental melancholy has again made him interesting to the twentieth century.*

from: *The Princess*
LYRIC

Now sleeps the crimson petal, now the white;
Nor waves the cypress in the palace walk;
Nor winks the gold fin in the porphyry font;
The fire-fly wakens: waken thou with me.

Now droops the milk-white peacock like a ghost,
And like a ghost she glimmers on to me.

Now lies the earth all Danaë to the stars,
And all thy heart lies open unto me.

Now slides the silent meteor on, and leaves
A shining furrow, as thy thoughts in me.

Now folds the lily all her sweetness up,
And slips into the bosom of the lake;
So fold thyself, my dearest, thou, and slip
Into my bosom and be lost in me.

from: *Ulysses*

I am become a name
For always roaming with a hungry heart;
Much have I seen and known; cities of men
And manners, climates, councils, governments,
Myself not least, but honour'd of them all;
And drunk delight of battle with my peers,
Far on the ringing plains of windy Troy.

from: *Locksley Hall*

For I dipt into the future, far as human eye could see,
Saw the Vision of the world, and all the wonder that would
  be;

Saw the heavens fill with commerce, argosies of magic sails,
Pilots of the purple twilight, dropping down with costly
  bales;

Heard the heavens fill with shouting, and there rain'd a
  ghastly dew
From the nations' airy navies grappling in the central
  blue; ...

Till the war-drum throbb'd no longer, and the battle-flags
  were furled
In the Parliament of man, the Federation of the world.

Crossing the Bar

Sunset and evening star,
  And one clear call for me!
And may there be no moaning of the bar,
  When I put out to sea.

But such a tide as moving seems asleep,
  Too full for sound and foam,
When that which drew from out the boundless deep
  Turns again home.

Twilight and evening bell,
  And after that the dark!
And may there be no sadness of farewell,
  When I embark;

For tho' from out our bourne of Time and Place
  The flood may bear me far,
I hope to see my Pilot face to face
  When I have crost the bar.

WILLIAM MAKEPEACE THACKERAY

(1811–1863)

Born in Calcutta, son of an employee of the East India Company, Thackeray was educated at Charterhouse and Trinity, Cambridge. He travelled, considered the bar, studied art in Paris and London, and finally settled for journalism, illustrating and literature. Writing for Punch *developed his wit, while the system of publishing novels in monthly numbers catered for his major works, such as* Vanity Fair *and* The Virginians. *Like Dickens he lectured in America; but whereas Dickens wept at his own fictional tragedies, Thackeray is likely to have laughed over his sallies at English sacred cows. Close neighbours in Poets' Corner, they were considered, rather unsubtly, to be contrasting geniuses, Dickens appealing more to the heart, Thackeray to the head.*

from: *Vanity Fair*

The Battle of Waterloo: Amelia is in Brussels, praying for her faithless husband George Osborne. George is on the field of battle.

Towards evening, the attack of the French, repeated and resisted so bravely, slackened in its fury. They had other foes besides the British to engage, or were preparing for a final onset. It came at last; the columns of the Imperial Guard marched up the hill of Saint Jean, at length and at once to sweep the English from the height which they had maintained all day, and spite of all; unscared by the thunder of the artillery, which hurled death from the English line – the dark rolling column pressed on and up the hill. It seemed almost to crest the eminence, when it began to waver and falter. Then it stopped, still facing the shot. Then at last the English troops rushed from the post from which no enemy had been able to dislodge them, and the Guard turned and fled.

No more firing was heard from Brussels – the pursuit rolled miles away. Darkness came down on the field and city; and Amelia

was praying for George, who was lying on his face, dead, with a
bullet through his heart.

from: BALLADS

Little Billee

Illustrated by Thackeray.

There were three sailors of Bristol city
Who took a boat and went to sea.
But first with beef and captain's biscuit
And pickled pork they loaded she.

There was gorging Jack and guzzling Jimmy,
And the youngest he was little Billee.
Now when they got as far as the Equator
They'd nothing left but one split pea.

Says gorging Jack to guzzling Jimmy,
'I am extremely hungaree.'
To gorging Jack says guzzling Jimmy,
'We've nothing left, us must eat we.' . . .

They tell little Billy they are going to eat him. He asks one last favour.

'First let me say my catechism,
Which my poor mammy taught to me.'
'Make haste, make haste,' says guzzling Jimmy,
While Jack pulled out his snickersnee.

Billy climbs up aloft, kneels – and sights land.

'Jerusalem and Madagascar,
And North and South Amerikee;
There's the British flag a-riding at anchor,
With Admiral Napier, KCB.'

So when they got aboard of the Admiral's
He hanged fat Jack and flogged Jimmee;
But as for little Bill he made him
The Captain of a Seventy-three.

from: *The Rose and the Ring*

*A 'fireside pantomime' for Christmas, illustrated, in which the usurper,
King Valoroso, his wife and daughter are punished by the Fairy Black-
stick. With the help of a magic rose and ring, the rightful heir, Prince
Giglio, is restored and marries the maid Betsinda, rightfully Princess
Rosalba.*

CHAPTER I

The Queen, after thinking whether she should go and see Giglio,
who had been sick, thought 'Not now. Business first; pleasure
afterwards. I will go and see dear Giglio this afternoon; and now
I will drive to the jewellers.' . . . The Princess went up into her
own room, and made Betsinda, her maid, bring out all her dresses
[*to bewitch the visiting Prince Bulbo*]; and as for Giglio, they forgot
him as much as I forget what I had for dinner last Tuesday
twelvemonth.

ROBERT BROWNING

(1812–1889)

*London born, Browning was the son of a bank clerk with an inviting
library, to which the boy eagerly responded. His career as a poet ran
smoothly – except when halted by the obscurities of his own sometimes
uncouth language. Sordello, a long narrative poem that curtailed his
fame for twenty years, was said to have only two intelligible lines, the
first and the last; and neither of them was true:*

Who will, may hear Sordello's story told. . . .
Who would has heard Sordello's story told.

Browning eventually recaptured his reputation, thanks to the energy of his style and the optimism of his thought. His famous elopement with and marriage to Elizabeth Barrett of Wimpole Street led to a happy life in Italy, until she died in 1861. By the eighties, soulful Victorian spouses were reading Browning aloud to each other and discussing his meaning. Rupert Brooke, the Great War poet, once joked that Browning managed to get the word 'God' into the last line of every poem.

from: *The Lost Leader*

The young, radical Wordsworth later supported the established order.

Just for a handful of silver he left us,
   Just for a riband to stick in his coat –
Found the one gift of which fortune bereft us,
   Lost all the others she lets us devote;
They, with the gold to give, doled him out silver,
   So much was theirs who so little allowed;
How all our copper had gone for his service!
   Rags – were they purple, his heart had been proud!
We that had loved him so, followed him, honoured him,
   Lived in his mild and magnificent eye,
Learned his great language, caught his clear accents,
   Made him our pattern to live and to die!
Shakespeare was of us, Milton was for us,
   Burns, Shelley, were with us, – they watch from their
      graves!
He alone breaks from the van and the freemen,
   He alone sinks to the rear and the slaves!

We shall march prospering, – not thro' his presence;
   Songs may inspirit us, – not from his lyre;
Deeds will be done, – while he boasts his quiescence,
   Still bidding crouch whom the rest bade aspire; . . .

Life's night begins; let him never come back to us!
  There would be doubt, hesitation and pain,
Forced praise on our part – the glimmer of twilight,
  Never glad confident morning again!
Best fight on well, for we taught him, – strike gallantly,
  Menace our heart ere we master his own;
Then let him receive the new knowledge and wait us,
  Pardoned in Heaven, the first by the throne!

from: *Rabbi Ben Ezra*

Grow old along with me!
The best is yet to be,
The last of life, for which the first was made;
Our times are in His hand
Who saith 'A whole I planned,
Youth shows but half; trust God: see all, nor be afraid!'

from: *Prospice*

Look forward.

Fear death? – to feel the fog in my throat,
  The mist in my face,
When the snows begin, and the blasts denote
  I am nearing the place,
The power of the night, the press of the storm,
  The post of the foe;
Where he stands, the Arch Fear in a visible form,
  Yet the strong man must go:
For the journey is done and the summit attained,
  And the barriers fall,
Though a battle's to fight ere the guerdon be gained,
  The reward of it all.
I was ever a fighter, so – one fight more,
  The best and the last!

I would hate that death bandaged my eyes, and forbore,
   And bade me creep past,
No! let me taste the whole of it, fare like my peers
   The heroes of old,
Bear the brunt, in a minute pay glad life's arrears
   Of pain, darkness and cold.
For sudden the worst turns the best to the brave,
   The black minute's at end,
And the elements' rage, the fiend-voices that rave,
   Shall dwindle, shall blend,
Shall change, shall become first a peace out of pain,
   Then a light, then thy breast,
O thou soul of my soul! I shall clasp thee again,
   And with God be the rest!

CHARLES DICKENS

(1812–1870)

Son of a naval pay clerk, Dickens was born in Portsmouth and moved to Chatham. His father's debts and his own labours in a blacking factory were reborn in David Copperfield. *The completed publication of* Pickwick Papers *in the first year of Queen Victoria's reign was to establish him as the prince of genial humour and British family life.* Household Words *seemed the right title for the weekly serialisation of his stories. He was boisterously creative. But the parting from his wife when he fell in love with the actress Ellen Ternan showed that the nation's idol was less exemplary than had been supposed. His gothic word-pictures of darkest London still harrow the imagination, while 'Uriah Heep' and 'Bill Sikes' continue to be sinister 'household words'. Dickens was a powerful reforming influence. In reading aloud from his own works he would reduce himself to tears of compassion. He and Thackeray are two of the prose giants of Poets' Corner.*

from: *Oliver Twist*

The hungry pauper boys in the parish institution have drawn lots, and young Oliver has got the short end: he is to ask for more.

The evening arrived; the boys took their places. The master, in his cook's uniform, stationed himself at the copper; his pauper assistants ranged themselves behind him; the gruel was served out; and a long grace was said over the short commons. The gruel disappeared; the boys whispered each other, and winked at Oliver; while his next neighbours nudged him. Child as he was, he was desperate with hunger, and reckless with misery. He rose from the table; and advancing to the master, basin and spoon in hand, said: somewhat alarmed at his own temerity:

'Please, sir, I want some more.'

The master was a fat, healthy man; but he turned very pale. He gazed in stupefied astonishment on the small rebel for some seconds, and then clung for support to the copper. The assistants were paralysed with wonder; the boys with fear.

'What!' said the master at length, in a faint voice.

'Please, sir,' replied Oliver, 'I want some more.'

The master aimed a blow at Oliver's head with the ladle; pinioned him in his arms; and shrieked aloud for the beadle.

The board were sitting in solemn conclave, when Mr Bumble rushed into the room in great excitement, and addressing the gentleman in the high chair, said,

'Mr Limbkins, I beg your pardon, sir! Oliver Twist has asked for more!'

There was a general start. Horror was depicted on every countenance.

'For *more*!' said Mr Limbkins. 'Compose yourself, Bumble, and answer me distinctly. Do I understand that he asked for more, after he had eaten the supper allotted by the dietary?'

'He did, sir,' replied Bumble.

'That boy will be hung,' said the gentleman in the white waistcoat. 'I know that boy will be hung.' . . .

For a week after the commission of the impious and profane offence of asking for more, Oliver remained a close prisoner in the dark and solitary room to which he had been consigned by the wisdom and mercy of the board.

After failing to apprentice him to a chimney-sweep, the board place Oliver with an undertaker. He escapes to London – and falls into the hands of Fagin and his gang of thieves.

from: *A Tale of Two Cities*

The beginning: The messenger from Tellson's Bank, travelling by night on the Dover coach, is haunted by the spectral memory of a Bastille victim, Dr Manette.

Yet even when his eyes were opened on the mist and rain, on the moving patch of light from the lamps, and the hedge at the road-side retreating by jerks, the night shadows outside the coach would fall into the train of the night shadows within. . . . Out of the midst of them the ghostly face would rise, and he would accost it again.
   'Buried how long?'
   'Almost eighteen years.'
   'I hope you care to live?'
   'I can't say.'
   Dig – dig – dig –

The novel ends with the debauched Sydney Carton about to give his life on the guillotine for Charles Darnay and Lucie Manette.

'It is a far, far better thing that I do than I have ever done; it is a far, far better rest that I go to than I have ever known.'

from: *Great Expectations*

Young Pip meets Miss Havisham, the woman who was abandoned years ago on her wedding day; she sits at her dressing-table.

In an arm-chair, with an elbow resting on the table and her head leaning on that hand, sat the strangest lady I have ever seen, or shall ever see.

She was dressed in rich materials – satins, and lace, and silks – all of white. Her shoes were white. And she had a long white veil dependent from her hair, but her hair was white. Some bright jewels sparkled on her neck and on her hands, and some other jewels lay sparkling on the table. Dresses, less splendid than the one she wore, and half-packed trunks were scattered about. She had not quite finished dressing, for she had but one shoe on – the other was on the table near her hand – her veil was but half arranged, her watch and chain were not put on. . . .

I saw that everything within view which ought to be white, had been white long ago, and had lost its lustre, and was faded and yellow. I saw that the bride within the bridal dress had withered like the dress, and like the flowers, and had no brightness left but the brightness of her sunken eyes. I saw that the dress had been put upon the rounded figure of a young woman, and that the figure upon which it now hung loose, had shrunk to skin and bone. . . .

It was when I stood before her, avoiding her eyes, that I took note of the surrounding objects in detail, and saw that her watch had stopped at twenty minutes to nine, and that a clock in the room had stopped at twenty minutes to nine. . . .

'Do you know what I touch here?' she said, laying her hands, one upon the other, on her left side.

'Yes, ma'am.' . . .

'What do I touch?'

'Your heart.'

'Broken!'

She uttered the word with an eager look, and with strong emphasis, and with a weird smile that had a kind of boast in it. Afterwards, she kept her hands there for a little while, and slowly took them away as if they were heavy.

'I am tired,' said Miss Havisham. 'I want diversion, and have done with men and women. Play.'

EDWARD LEAR

(1812–1888)

Twentieth child of a London stockbroker, Lear always lacked robust health (epileptic and depressive) while possessing brilliant and varied talents. He taught drawing to the royal family in 1845, and thanks to his patron, Lord Derby, was able to travel and sketch assiduously. Derby's grandchildren were the first to enjoy Lear's nonsense world. This included nonsense rhymes about real and invented animals (at nineteen he was a draughtsman in the London Zoo); nonsense pictures, including botanical specimens such as the orchid-like Many Peoplia Upsidedownia; *and nonsense cookery. His last years were spent in San Remo, for his health and his painting.*

The Owl and the Pussy-cat

The Owl and the Pussy-cat went to sea
In a beautiful pea-green boat,
They took some honey, and plenty of money,
Wrapped up in a 5-pound note.
The Owl looked up to the stars above,
And sang to a small guitar,
'O lovely Pussy! O Pussy, my love,
What a beautiful Pussy you are,
 You are,
 You are!
What a beautiful Pussy you are!'

Pussy said to the Owl, 'You elegant fowl!
How charmingly sweet you sing!
O let us be married! too long we have tarried:
But what shall we do for a ring?'
They sailed away, for a year and a day,
To the land where the Bong-tree grows,

And there in a wood a Piggy-wig stood
With a ring through the end of his nose,
  His nose,
  His nose,
With a ring through the end of his nose.

'Dear Pig, are you willing to sell for one shilling
Your ring?' Said the Piggy, 'I will.'
So they took it away, and were married next day
By the Turkey who lives on the hill.
They dined on mince, and slices of quince,
Which they ate with a runcible spoon;
And hand in hand, on the edge of the sand,
They danced by the light of the moon,
  The moon,
  The moon,
They danced by the light of the moon.

from: NONSENSE COOKERY

To Make an Amblongus Pie

Take 4 pounds (say 4½ pounds) of fresh Amblongusses, and put
them in a small pipkin. Cover them with water and boil them for
8 hours incessantly. ... When you have ascertained that the
Amblongusses are quite soft ... place them in a wide pan (adding
nutmeg, powdered gingerbread, curry-powder, cayenne pepper).
Remove the pan into the next room, and place it on the floor.
Bring it back again, and let it simmer for three-quarters of an
hour. ... Then, having prepared the paste, insert the whole
carefully, adding ... a small pigeon, 2 slices of beef, 4 cauli-
flowers, and any number of oysters. Watch patiently till the crust
begins to rise. ... Serve up in a clean dish, and throw the whole
out of the window as fast as possible.

CHARLOTTE BRONTË

(1816–1855)

Eldest surviving daughter of the Revd Patrick Brontë, Charlotte spent almost her whole life at Haworth Parsonage, between Bradford and her bleak beloved Yorkshire moors. From both her parents she inherited Celtic blood: Irish from Patrick, Cornish from Maria Branwell, her mother. She and her only brother, Branwell, wrote the secret Angria *saga as children. After wretched experiences at school and governessing, Charlotte and her sister Emily studied French at the Pensionat Héger in Brussels, hoping to teach young ladies at the Parsonage. No young Ladies applied; but the result was Charlotte's falling in love with M Constantin Héger, a drama celebrated in* Villette. *In order to support Branwell (a potential artist but drunkard and opium-eater who died at thirty-one) Charlotte published the poems of herself and her sisters under the sexless pen names of Currer, Ellis and Acton Bell. Only two copies sold; but* Jane Eyre *followed, becoming a bestseller. In* Jane, *Charlotte created a governess who could fight back and a woman who could show as well as inspire passion. When all her siblings were dead the lonely Charlotte became Mrs Arthur Bell Nicholls by marrying her father's curate. (Thus she twice took his name.) She died, probably from tuberculosis made rampant by pregnancy.*

On the Death of Emily Brontë

Written five days afterwards.

> My darling, thou wilt never know
> The grinding agony of woe
>   That we have borne for thee.
> Thus may we consolation tear
> E'en from the depth of our despair
>   And wasting misery.

The nightly anguish thou art spared
When all the crushing truth is bared
   To the awakening mind,
When the galled heart is pierced with grief,
Till wildly it implores relief,
   But small relief can find.

Nor know'st thou what it is to lie
Looking forth with streaming eye
   On life's lone wilderness.
Weary, weary, dark and drear,
How shall I the journey bear,
   The burden and distress?

Then since thou art spared such pain
We will not wish thee here again;
   He that lives must mourn.
God help us through our misery
And give us rest and joy with thee
   When we reach our bourne!

from: *Jane Eyre*

The mysterious, sardonic Mr Rochester requires a governess for his young ward. He employs Jane, who falls in love with him. In Rochester Charlotte Brontë had created the new type of Byronic hero that was to thrill and shock the Victorian world.

My master's colourless, olive face, square, massive brow, broad and jetty eyebrows, deep eyes, strong features, firm, grim mouth, – all energy, decision, will, – were not beautiful, according to rule; but they were more than beautiful to me: they were full of an interest, an influence that quite mastered me, – that took my feelings from my own power and fettered them in his. I had not intended to love him: the reader knows I had wrought hard to extirpate from my soul the germs of love there detected; and now, at the first renewed view of him, they spontaneously revived, green and strong! He made me love him without looking at me.

EMILY JANE BRONTË

(1818–1848)

The most striking yet most enigmatic of the three sisters, Emily was always unreservedly happy at desolate Haworth but desperately homesick everywhere else. Her short stays at boarding schools and at the Belgian pensionat with Charlotte were emotional disasters, for her interior life collapsed. This life seems to have had two facets: the fictional land of Gondal, *with its romantic adventures that she and Anne, her younger sister, together invented; and her mystical visions that, like* Gondal, *inspired her poetry. Her only novel,* Wuthering Heights, *impassioned and at times mysterious, had to wait till after Emily's death – from the dread consumption – for acclaim. It is famous for, among other things, the characters of Cathy and the neo-Byronic Heathcliff, who each has 'a chainless soul', like Emily herself.*

from: GONDAL

The Prisoner

'Still let my tyrants know, I am not doomed to wear
Year after year in gloom, and desolate despair;
A messenger of Hope comes every night to me,
And offers for short life, eternal liberty.

'He comes with western winds, with evening's wandering
  airs,
With that clear dusk of heaven that brings the thickest stars,
Winds take a pensive tone, and stars a tender fire,
And visions rise, and change, that kill me with desire.

'Desire for nothing known in my maturer years,
When Joy grew mad with awe, at counting future tears.
When, if my spirit's sky was full of flashes warm,
I knew not whence they came, from sun or thunder storm.

'But, first, a hush of peace – a soundless calm descends;
The struggle of distress, and fierce impatience ends;
Mute music soothes my breast – unuttered harmony,
That I could never dream, till Earth was lost to me.

'Then dawns the Invisible; the Unseen its truth reveals;
My outward sense is gone, my inward essence feels:
Its wings are almost free – its home, its harbour found,
Measuring the gulf, it stoops and dares the final bound.

'O dreadful is the check – intense the agony –
When the ear begins to hear, and the eye begins to see;
When the pulse begins to throb, the brain to think again;
The soul to feel the flesh, and the flesh to feel the chain.

'Yet I would lose no sting, would wish no torture less;
The more that anguish racks, the earlier it will bless;
And robed in fires of hell, or bright with heavenly shine,
If it but herald death, the vision is divine!'

Last Lines

No coward soul is mine,
No trembler in the world's storm-troubled sphere;
I see Heaven's glories shine,
And faith shines equal, arming me from fear.

O God within my breast,
Almighty, ever-present Deity!
Life – that in me has rest,
As I – undying Life – have power in Thee!

Vain are the thousand creeds
That move men's hearts: unalterably vain;
Worthless as withered weeds,
Or idlest froth amid the boundless main,

To waken doubt in one
Holding so fast by Thine infinity;
So surely anchored on
The steadfast rock of immortality.

With wide-embracing love
The spirit animates eternal years,
Pervades and broods above,
Changes, sustains, dissolves, creates, and rears.

Though earth and man were gone,
And suns and universes cease to be,
And Thou wert left alone,
Every existence would exist in Thee.

There is no room for Death,
Nor atom that his might could render void:
Thou – Thou art Being and Breath,
And what Thou art may never be destroyed.

from: *Wuthering Heights*

The narrator is Mr Lockwood, former tenant of Thrushcross Grange,
near Wuthering Heights.

I sought, and soon discovered, the three headstones on the slope
next the moor: the middle one grey, and half buried in heath:
Edgar Linton's only harmonised by the turf and moss creeping
up its foot; Heathcliff's still bare.

I lingered round them, under that benign sky: watched the
moths fluttering among the heath and harebells, listened to the
soft wind breathing through the grass, and wondered how any
one could ever imagine unquiet slumbers for the sleepers in that
quiet earth.

ANNE BRONTË

(1820–1849)

Youngest of this extraordinary family, Anne was brought up by their Aunt Branwell, who drummed into her niece her own stern religion of salvation and damnation. The melancholy it induced was mitigated when Anne received a sick visit at boarding school from a Moravian bishop preaching divine love. She experienced human love for the Revd Willie Weightman, her father's handsome curate, but he died of cholera. Her imagination, though less powerful than her sisters', was stimulated by three experiences: her own ambivalent career as governess, re-created in her novel Agnes Grey, *the* Gondal *stories she shared with Emily, and her brother's real-life drama, partly responsible for* The Tenant of Wildfell Hall. *She died at Scarborough of consumption, supported by Charlotte.*

from: *Severed and Gone*

In fifteen stanzas, Anne remembers Willie Weightman.

Severed and gone, so many years,
　　And art thou still so dear to me,
That throbbing heart and burning tears
　　Can witness how I clung to thee? . . .

Had I one treasured lock of thine,
　　How it would bless these longing eyes!
Or if thy pictured form were mine,
　　What gold should rob me of the prize? . . .

Thou breathest in my bosom yet,
　　And dwellest in my beating heart;
And while I cannot quite forget,
　　Thou, darling, canst not quite depart.

Life seems more sweet that thou didst live,
 And men more true that thou wert one;
Nothing is lost that thou didst give,
 Nothing destroyed that thou hast done.

GEORGE ELIOT

(1819–1880)

Daughter of a Warwickshire land agent, Mary Ann Evans, later known as George Eliot, was devoted to her brother Isaac, who disapproved of her unconventional life; he caused her permanent distress without achieving 'reform'. Mary Ann had no need to adopt a male pseudonym in order to be recognised as a superlatively great novelist. But emotional profundity and brilliant intellect were generally associated with the male mind. Though she lived with the philosopher G. H. Lewes, a married man whom she called 'husband', Victorian royalty were glad to meet her. After Lewes's death, she married John Cross, twenty-one years her junior. Perhaps fortunately for Cross, she died a few months later – for marriage to the formidable guru was no light undertaking. He wrote her Life, *which was easier than living in it.*

from: *Brother and Sister*

The first poem in a sequence of eleven, written by George Eliot in later life.

He was the elder and a little man
Of forty inches, bound to show no dread,
And I the girl that puppy-like now ran,
Now lagged behind my brother's larger tread.

I held him wise, and when he talked to me
Of snakes and birds, and which God loved the best,
I thought his knowledge marked the boundary
Where men grew blind, though angels knew the rest.

If he said 'Hush!' I tried to hold my breath,
Wherever he said 'Come!' I stepped in faith.

from: *The Mill on the Floss*

The sister and brother, Maggie and Tom Tulliver, are drowned in the flooded River Floss.

. . . a new danger was being carried towards them by the river. Some wooden machinery had just given way on one of the wharves, and huge fragments were being floated along. The sun was rising now, and the wide area of watery desolation was spread out in dreadful clearness around them – in dreadful clearness floated onwards the hurrying, threatening masses. A large company in a boat that was working its way along under the Tofton houses, observed their danger and shouted, 'Get out of the current!'

But that could not be done at once, and Tom, looking before him, saw death rushing on them. Huge fragments, clinging together in fatal fellowship, made one wide mass across the stream.

'It is coming, Maggie!' Tom said in a deep hoarse voice, loosing the oars, and clasping her.

The next instant the boat was no longer seen upon the water – and the huge mass was hurrying on in hideous triumph.

But soon the keel of the boat reappeared, a black speck on the golden water.

The boat reappeared – but brother and sister had gone down in an embrace never to be parted: living through again in one supreme moment the days when they had clasped their little hands in love, and roamed the daisied fields together.

CONCLUSION

Nature repairs her ravages – repairs them with her sunshine, and with human labour. The desolation wrought by that flood, had left little visible trace on the face of the earth, five years after.

The fifth autumn was rich in golden corn-stacks, rising in thick clusters among the distant hedge-rows; the wharves and warehouses on the Floss were busy again, with echoes of eager voices, with hopeful lading and unlading. . . .

Nature repairs her ravages – but not all. The up-torn trees are not rooted again; the parted hills are left scarred: if there is a new growth, the trees are not the same as the old, and the hills underneath their green vesture bear the marks of the past rending. To the eyes that have dwelt on the past, there is no thorough repair.

JOHN RUSKIN

(1819–1900)

The only child of a wealthy Surrey wine-merchant who recognised his son's precocity in the arts, young Ruskin was taken travelling through Europe. He came to glorify Gothic architecture and detest the Renaissance. He lectured, wrote and illustrated extensively. One of his lectures sent the youthful Cecil Rhodes out to found Rhodesia (Zimbabwe). He visualised a better world for the working-man, based on Christian values; not greed. A prophet to some, to others he was an intemperate dogmatist. With women he was immature rather than precocious: Effie Gray, his wife, divorced him for impotence and at forty-seven he was infatuated with an eighteen-year-old. He died at Brantwood on Coniston Water, cherished by his cousin Joan Severn.

from: *The Stones of Venice*
VOLUME I CHAPTER ONE: THE QUARRY

Since first the dominion of men was asserted over the ocean, three thrones, of mark beyond all others, have been set upon its sands: the thrones of Tyre, Venice and England. Of the first of these great powers only the memory remains; of the second, the ruin; the third, which inherits their greatness, if it forget their example, may be led through prouder eminence to less pitiful destruction.

The exaltation, the sin, and the punishment of Tyre have been recorded for us, in perhaps the most touching words ever uttered by the Prophets of Israel against the cities of the stranger. But we read them as a lovely song; for the very depth of the Fall of Tyre has blinded us to its reality, and we forget, as we watch the bleaching of the rocks between the sunshine and the sea, that they were once 'as in Eden, the garden of God.'

Her successor, like her in perfection of beauty, though less in endurance of dominion, is still left for our beholding in the final period of her decline: a ghost upon the sands of the sea, so weak – so quiet, – so bereft of all but her loveliness, that we might well doubt, as we watched her faint reflection in the mirage of the lagoon, which was the City and which the Shadow.

I would endeavour to trace the lines of this image before it be for ever lost, and to record, as far as I may, the warning which seems to me to be uttered by every one of the fast-gaining waves, that beat like passing bells, against the STONES OF VENICE.

from: *The Crown of Wild Olive*

A collection of lectures, this one delivered in the town hall of Bradford, Yorkshire.

Change *must* come; but it is ours to determine whether change of growth, or change of death. Shall the Parthenon be in ruins on its rock, and Bolton priory in its meadow, but these mills of yours be the consummation of the buildings of the earth, and their wheels be as the wheels of eternity? Think you that 'men may come, and men may go,' but – mills – go on for ever? Not so; out of these, better or worse shall come; and it is for you to choose which.

I know that none of this wrong is done with deliberate purpose. [The 'wrong' of greed and inordinate possessions.] I know, on the contrary, that you wish your workmen well; that you do much for them, and that you desire to do more for them, if you saw your way to such benevolence safely. I know that even all this wrong and misery are brought about by a warped sense of duty, each of you striving to do his best; but, unhappily, not knowing for whom this best should be done. And all our hearts have been betrayed by the plausible impiety of the modern economist, telling us that, 'To do the best for ourselves, is finally to do the best for others.' Friends, our great Master said not so; and most absolutely we shall find this world is not made so. Indeed, to do the best for others, is finally to do the best for ourselves; but it will not do to have our eyes fixed on that issue. The Pagans had got beyond that.

Ruskin goes on to argue that Plato, in his idealised picture of early Athens, said the people cared little for gold, provided there was 'common love and virtue'. The mill-owners of Bradford had wanted Ruskin's advice on building a new Exchange. They got an unexpected answer:

... this idol of riches; this idol of yours; this golden image, high by measureless cubits, set up where your green fields of England are furnace-burnt into the likeness of the plain of Dura: this idol, forbidden to us, first of all idols, by our own Master and faith; forbidden to us also by every human lip that has ever, in any age or people, been accounted of as able to speak according to the purposes of God. Continue to make that forbidden deity your principal one, and soon no more art, no more science, no more pleasure will be possible. Catastrophe will come; or, worse than catastrophe, slow mouldering and withering into Hades. But if you can fix some conception of a true human state of life to be striven for – life, good for all men, as for yourselves; ... – then, and so sanctifying wealth into 'commonwealth', all your art, your literature, your daily labours, your domestic affection, and citizen's duty, will join and increase into one magnificent harmony. You will know then how to build, well enough; you will build with stone well, but with flesh better; temples not made with hands, but riveted of hearts; and that kind of marble, crimson-veined, is indeed eternal.

MATTHEW ARNOLD

(1822–1888)

With this member of the Arnold family we find ourselves among one of the greatest English literary clans. Eldest son of the formidable 'Arnold (headmaster) of Rugby', Matthew Arnold's connections by blood and marriage were to include the Wards, Huxleys, Trevelyans, Arnold-Forsters. Arnold's life divides into halves: first the poet; second the critic, educationist and school inspector. No one has more poignantly expressed his era's loss of religious certainties. In his poem, 'The Scholar Gipsy', Arnold calls on the Oxford scholars of his own day to 'fly our paths, our feverish contact fly!' – just as the legendary scholar gipsy of two hundred years ago fled from 'the line of festal light in Christ-Church hall'. The eternal academic in Arnold made him try to extract a lesson everywhere and from everything; Shakespeare alone would not speak to him in precepts – nor did he need to flee the world, being already alone.

Shakespeare

Others abide our question. Thou art free.
We ask and ask: Thou smilest and art still,
Out-topping knowledge. For the loftiest hill
That to the stars uncrowns his majesty,
Planting his steadfast footsteps in the sea,
Making the Heaven of Heavens his dwelling-place,
Spares but the cloudy border of his base
To the foil'd searching of mortality:
And thou, who didst the stars and sunbeams know,
Self-school'd, self-scann'd, self-honour'd, self-secure,
Didst walk on earth unguess'd at. Better so!
All pains the immortal spirit must endure,
   All weakness that impairs, all griefs that bow,
   Find their sole voice in that victorious brow.

from: *Thyrsis*

ON THE DEATH OF
ARTHUR HUGH CLOUGH, 1861

*Arnold is retracing the steps that he and Clough took together as students
at Oxford.*

Runs it not here, the track by Childsworth Farm,
    Up past the wood, to where the elm-tree crowns
      The hill behind whose ridge the sunset flames?
The signal-elm, that looks on Ilsley Downs,
     The Vale, the three lone weirs, the youthful Thames? –
      This winter-eve is warm,
Humid the air, leafless, yet soft as spring,
    The tender purple spray on copse and briers;
    And that sweet City with her dreaming spires,
She needs not June for beauty's heightening.

from: *Dover Beach*

The sea is calm to-night,
The tide is full, the moon lies fair
Upon the straits: – on the French coast, the light
Gleams, and is gone; the cliffs of England stand,
Glimmering and vast, out in the tranquil bay.
Come to the window, sweet is the night air!

Only, from the long line of spray
Where the sea meets the moon-blanch'd land,
Listen! you hear the grating roar
Of pebbles which the waves draw back, and fling,
At their return, up the high strand,
Begin, and cease, and then again begin,
With tremulous cadence slow, and bring
The eternal note of sadness in. . . .

The sea of faith
Was once, too, at the full, and round earth's shore
Lay like the folds of a bright girdle furl'd;
But now I only hear
Its melancholy, long, withdrawing roar,
Retreating, to the breath
Of the night-wind down the vast edges drear
And naked shingles of the world.

Ah, love, let us be true
To one another! for the world, which seems
To lie before us like a land of dreams,
So various, so beautiful, so new,
Hath really neither joy, nor love, nor light,
Nor certitude, nor peace, nor help for pain;
And we are here as on a darkling plain
Swept with confused alarms of struggle and flight,
Where ignorant armies clash by night.

West London

Crouch'd on the pavement close by Belgrave Square
A tramp I saw, ill, moody, and tongue-tied;
A babe was in her arms, and at her side
A girl; their clothes were rags, their feet were bare.

Some labouring men, whose work lay somewhere there,
Pass'd opposite; she touch'd her girl, who hied
Across, and begg'd, and came back satisfied.
The rich she had let pass with frozen stare.

Thought I: above her state this spirit towers;
She will not ask of aliens but of friends,
Of sharers in a common human fate.

She turns from that cold succour, which attends
The unknown little from the unknowing great,
And points us to a better time than ours.

LEWIS CARROLL

(1832–1898)

As a lecturer in mathematics at Christ Church, Oxford, the Revd Charles Lutwidge Dodgson (Lewis Carroll) discovered his gift for amusing little girls with a tale of mad logic; also his need for their company as audience for his stories and subjects for his photography. Alice in Wonderland *originated in a boat trip on the river with Dean Liddell's three daughters, Alice being the middle one. Their father had been allowed to marry and have a family because he was Dean; Dodgson was forbidden by the Victorian rules – unless he resigned his fellowship of the college.* Alice *and its sequel* Through the Looking-glass *were as necessary to the bachelor don as they were, and are, to generations of children.*

from: *Alice in Wonderland*

The Caterpillar tells Alice to recite 'You are old Father William' to test her memory. It comes out all wrong.

'You are old, Father William,' the young man said,
　'And your hair has become very white;
And yet you incessantly stand on your head -
　Do you think, at your age, it is right?'

'In my youth', Father William replied to his son,
　'I feared it might injure the brain;
But, now that I'm perfectly sure I have none,
　Why, I do it again and again.'

'You are old,' said the youth, 'as I mentioned before,
　And have grown most uncommonly fat;
Yet you turned a back-somersault in at the door –
　Pray, what is the reason of that?'

'In my youth,' said the sage, as he shook his grey locks,
  'I kept all my limbs very supple
By the use of this ointment – one shilling the box –
  Allow me to sell you a couple?'

'You are old,' said the youth, 'and your jaws are too weak
  For anything tougher than suet;
Yet you finished the goose, with the bones and the beak –
  Pray, how did you manage to do it?'

'In my youth,' said his father, 'I took to the law,
  And argued each case with my wife;
And the muscular strength, which it gave to my jaw
  Has lasted the rest of my life.'

'You are old,' said the youth, 'one would hardly suppose
  That your eye was as steady as ever;
Yet you balanced an eel on the end of your nose –
  What made you so awfully clever?'

'I have answered three questions, and that is enough,'
  Said his father. 'Don't give yourself airs!
Do you think I can listen all day to such stuff?
  Be off, or I'll kick you down-stairs!'

ADAM LINDSAY GORDON

(1833–1870)

Born in the Azores where his father, a retired Indian officer, had temporarily settled, Gordon was too high-spirited and addicted to sport (boxing, racing) for English schooling or indeed England to tie him down. He emigrated to Australia at twenty, where his true adventurous life began. A daring horse-breaker and friend of the bushmen, he was elected to Parliament at thirty-one; but speeches bored him. He soon returned to steeplechasing and poetry, having already won in Adelaide and published in Melbourne. Gordon had married in 1862. Domestic responsibility and a see-saw of successes and debts caused him anxiety. He suffered from what has been called 'manly melancholy' and shot himself. His poetry, all composed out of doors, was said to be 'the voice of Australia'. He carried a Horace *in his pocket, loved to quote Byron and Scott, and is the first Australian poet to be honoured in Westminster.*

from: *Ye Wearie Wayfarer*

Whisper, spring-wind, softly singing,
    Whisper in my ear;
Respite and nepenthe bringing,
    Can the goal be near?
Laden with the dew of vespers,
    From the fragrant sky,
In my ear the wind that whispers
    Seems to make reply –

'Question not, but live and labour
    Till yon goal be won,
Helping every feeble neighbour,
    Seeking help from none;
Life is mostly froth and bubble,
    Two things stand like stone,
Kindness in another's trouble,
    Courage in your own.' . . .

from: *Hippodromania*

There's a lull in the tumult on yonder hill,
    And the clamour has grown less loud,
Though the Babel of tongues is never still,
    With the presence of such a crowd.

The bell has rung. With their riders up
    At the starting-post they muster,
The racers stripped for the 'Melbourne Cup',
    All gloss and polish and lustre;
And the course is seen with its emerald sheen,
    By the bright spring-tide renewed,
Like a ribbon of green, stretched out between
    The ranks of the multitude.

The flag is lowered. 'They're off!' 'They come!'
    The squadron is sweeping on;
A sway in the crowd – a murmuring hum:
    'They're here!' 'They're past!' 'They're gone!'
They came with the rush of the southern surf,
    On the bar of the storm-girt bay;
And like muffled drums on the sounding turf
    Their hoof-strokes echo away.

THOMAS HARDY

(1840–1928)

Son of a Wessex stonemason, Hardy became an outstanding poet, as well as the better-known creator of 'Tess' and 'Jude'. His lyrics, short nature poems, philosophical pieces and long dramatic works make up a huge 'Collected Poems' of nearly 1,000 pages. Though Hardy's first marriage was unhappy (perhaps due to hypergamy – stonemason's son wedded to Cornish vicar's sister-in-law) he seems to have regretted his wife's death in 1912. His second wife combined with his terrier to repulse intruders from his home. Despite his pessimistic view of man's fate on earth, he was awarded many honours including the Order of Merit.

When I Set Out for Lyonnesse

When I set out for Lyonnesse
  A hundred miles away,
    The rime was on the spray,
And starlight lit my lonesomeness
When I set out for Lyonnesse
  A hundred miles away.

What would bechance at Lyonnesse
  While I should sojourn there
    No prophet durst declare
Nor did the wisest wizard guess
What would bechance at Lyonnesse
  While I should sojourn there.

When I came back from Lyonnesse
  With magic in my eyes,
    All marked with mute surmise
My radiance rare and fathomless,
When I came back from Lyonnesse
  With magic in my eyes.

The Young Glass-stainer

'These Gothic windows, how they wear me out
With cusp and foil, and nothing straight or square,
Crude colours, leaden borders round about,
And fitting in Peter here, and Matthew there!

'What a vocation! Here do I draw now
The abnormal, loving the Hellenic norm;
Martha I paint, and dream of Hera's brow,
Mary, and think of Aphrodite's form.'

Afternoon Service at Mellstock

c. 1850.

On afternoons of drowsy calm
We stood in the panelled pew,
Singing one-voiced a Tate-and-Brady psalm
To the tune of 'Cambridge New'.

We watched the elms, we watched the rooks,
The clouds upon the breeze,
Between the while of glancing at our books,
And swaying like the trees.

So mindless were those outpourings! –
Though I am not aware
That I have gained by subtle thought on things
Since we stood psalming there.

The Oxen

1915.

Christmas Eve, and twelve of the clock.
'Now they are all on their knees,'
An elder said as we sat in a flock
By the embers in hearthside ease.

We pictured the meek mild creatures where
They dwelt in their strawy pen,
Nor did it occur to one of us there
To doubt they were kneeling then.

So fair a fancy few would weave
In these years! Yet, I feel,
If someone said on Christmas Eve,
'Come; see the oxen kneel

'In the lonely barton by yonder coomb
Our childhood used to know,'
I should go with him in the gloom
Hoping it might be so.

HENRY JAMES

(1843–1916)

*Born in New York and naturalised British in 1915, James was one of
the distinguished writers (awarded the Order of Merit shortly before
his death) not born British who entered Poets' Corner. He wrote with
great perceptiveness of American and English human nature. His subtle
knowledge of the latter was gained from living in London and lovely
Lamb House, Rye. His brilliant and intricate novella about the beautiful
English house called Poynton shows the upper-class male as 'stupid',
'honest' and 'handsome', while the dependent female is absurdly self-
sacrificing – yet neither is unsympathetically so. James's father and elder
brother were philosophers of religion.*

from: *The Spoils of Poynton*

*Two love stories are here intertwined. First, the obsessive love of Mrs
Gereth for the exquisite and extremely valuable contents of her house,
Poynton, which she collected as a wife, but as a widow must see legally
left to her son Owen and his vulgar rapacious future wife, Mona Brigstock, who lives at neighbouring Waterbath. (Only the English could
tolerate such a procedure.) Secondly, the love of Mrs Gereth's enchanting
penniless companion, Fleda Vetch, for Owen and his for her. In the
following passage we know that the over-scrupulous Fleda has insisted
on the weak Owen going personally to Waterbath to break off his
engagement to Mona. Why have Fleda and Mrs Gereth heard nothing
from him since? We also know that Mrs Gereth, after illegally removing
the 'spoils' from Poynton to prevent Mona getting them, has now
returned them, she thinks into Fleda's safe hands.*

'You plunge me in stupefaction,' [Mrs Gereth answered Fleda,] 'and at the same time you terrify me. Your account of Owen's inconceivable, and yet I don't know what to hold on by. He cares for you, it does appear, and yet in the same breath you tell me that nothing is more possible than that he's spending these days at Waterbath. Pardon me if I'm so dull as not to see my way in such darkness. If he's at Waterbath he doesn't care for you. If he cares for you he's not at Waterbath.'

'Then where is he?' poor Fleda helplessly wailed. She caught herself up, however; she would do her best to be brave and clear. Before Mrs Gereth could reply ... [Fleda] found an air of assurance to say: 'You simplify far too much. You always did and you always will. The tangle of life is much more intricate than you've ever, I think, felt it to be. You slash into it,' cried Fleda finely, 'with a great pair of shears; you nip at it as if you were one of the Fates! If Owen's at Waterbath he's there to wind everything up.'

His mother shook her head with slow austerity. 'You don't believe a word you're saying. I've frightened you, as you've frightened me: you're whistling in the dark to keep up our courage. I do simplify, doubtless, if to simplify is to fail to comprehend the inanity of a passion that bewilders a young blockhead [Owen] with bugaboo barriers, with hideous and monstrous sacrifices. I can only repeat that you're beyond me. Your perversity's a thing to howl over. However,' the poor woman continued with a break in her voice, a long hesitation and then the dry triumph of her will, 'I'll never mention it to you again! Owen I can just make out; for Owen *is* a blockhead. Owen's a blockhead,' she repeated with a quiet tragic finality, looking straight into Fleda's eyes. 'I don't know why you dress up so the fact that he's disgustingly weak.'

Fleda at last, before her companion's, lowered her look. 'Because I love him. It's because he's weak that he needs me,' she added.

'That was why his father, whom he exactly resembles, needed *me*. And I didn't fail his father,' said Mrs Gereth. She gave her visitor a moment to appreciate the remark; after which she pursued: 'Mona Brigstock isn't weak. She's stronger than you!'

'I never thought she was weak,' Fleda answered. She looked vaguely round the room with a new purpose: she had lost sight of her umbrella.

'I did tell you to let yourself go, but it's clear enough that you really haven't,' Mrs Gereth declared. 'If Mona has got him –'

Fleda had accomplished her search; her hostess paused. 'If Mona has got him?' the girl panted, tightening the umbrella.

'Well,' said Mrs Gereth profoundly, 'it will be clear enough that Mona *has*.'

'Has let herself go?'

'Has let herself go.' Mrs Gereth spoke as if she meant it to the fullest extent of her cynicism and saw it in every detail.

Mona of course had recaptured Owen and the 'spoils'; but a few months later Poynton was mysteriously burnt to the ground.

GERARD MANLEY HOPKINS

(1844–1889)

Hopkins was born at Stratford, Essex, to comfortably off, High-Anglican parents. After boarding at Highgate school, he took a (classical) first at Balliol College, Oxford and entered the Roman Catholic Church. He became a Jesuit and in 1877 was ordained. Around this date he wrote some of his finest poetry. His training in Wales was happy but his frail physique was strained by parish work in poverty-stricken Liverpool and he was lonely as Professor of Classics in Dublin, where he died, probably of typhoid. Hopkins, says his biographer R. B. Martin, believed in 'the unity of man and nature as parts of Divine creation'. He coined the innovative phrase 'sprung rhythm' (beat rather than counted syllables, the nearest thing to ordinary speech) and the mysterious 'inscape' and 'instress' (concerned with essence and unity in created things). Today his influence outstrips that of his contemporaries.

from: *The Wreck of the Deutschland*

TO THE HAPPY MEMORY OF FIVE FRANCISCAN NUNS, EXILES BY THE
FALCK LAWS FROM GERMANY: DROWNED BETWEEN MIDNIGHT
AND MORNING OF DEC. 7TH, 1875

*Hopkins felt himself an exile from his home and family because of their
lack of sympathy with his religion.*

> Away in the loveable west,
>   On a pastoral forehead of Wales,
> I was under a roof here, I was at rest,
>   And they the prey of the gales;
> She to the black-about air, to the breaker, the thickly
> Falling flakes, to the throng that catches and quails
>   Was calling 'O Christ, Christ, come quickly':
> The cross to her she calls Christ to her, christens her
>   wild-worst Best.

God's Grandeur

> The world is charged with the grandeur of God.
>   It will flame out, like shining from shook foil;
>   It gathers to a greatness, like the ooze of oil[1]
> Crushed. Why do men then now not reck his rod?
> Generations have trod, have trod, have trod;
>   And all is seared with trade; bleared, smeared with toil;
>   And wears man's smudge and shares man's smell: the soil
> Is bare now, nor can foot feel, being shod.
>
> And for all this, nature is never spent;
>   There lives the dearest freshness deep down things;
> And though the last lights off the black West went
>   Oh, morning, at the brown brink eastward, springs –
> Because the Holy Ghost over the bent
>   World broods with warm breast and with ah! bright
>   wings.

[1] Olive oil.

Pied Beauty

Glory be to God for dappled things –
  For skies of couple-colour as a brinded cow;
    For rose-moles all in stipple upon trout that swim;
Fresh-firecoal chestnut falls; finches' wings;
  Landscape plotted and pieced – fold, fallow, and plough;
  And all trades, their gear and tackle and trim.

All things counter,[1] original, spare, strange;
  Whatever is fickle, freckled (who knows how?)
    With swift, slow; sweet, sour; adazzle, dim;
He fathers-forth, whose beauty is past change:
                    Praise him.

from: *Binsey, Oxford Poplars*
FELLED 1879

My aspens dear, whose airy cages quelled,
Quelled or quenched in leaves the leaping sun,
All felled, felled, are all felled;
  Of a fresh and following folded rank
    Not spared, not one
    That dandled a sandalled[2]
  Shadow that swam or sank
On meadow and river and wind-wandering
  weed-winding bank.

[1] Contrasting, original, unique.
[2] Interlaced.

RUDYARD KIPLING

(1865–1936)

Kipling's parentage was more distinguished than that of many other poets in the 'Corner'. Born in Bombay, he had a successful writer and illustrator for a father, while his mother was the sister-in-law of the painter Sir Edward Burne-Jones. Two relatively recent events combined to downgrade his poetry, at least temporarily. His death coincided with that of King George V, so that, according to his friends, he glided almost unnoticed into oblivion. More important was the death of the British Empire soon after Kipling's. As a reputed hardline Imperialist, he fell into disfavour as a poet. In reality his journalistic and literary work in India showed him to be a descriptive and imaginative writer of genius, while his writings about Sussex, where he settled at Bateman's, are evocative of local history. He won the Nobel Prize for Literature, the first Englishman to do so.

from: PUCK OF POOK'S HILL

A Smugglers' Song

If you wake at midnight, and hear a horse's feet,
Don't go drawing back the blind, or looking in the street,
Them that asks no questions isn't told a lie,
Watch the wall, my darling, while the Gentlemen go by!
　　Five and twenty ponies,
　　Trotting through the dark –
　　Brandy for the Parson,
　　'Baccy for the Clerk;
　　Laces for a lady; letters for a spy,
And watch the wall, my darling, while the Gentlemen go
　　by!

L'Envoi

When Earth's last picture is painted and the tubes are
   twisted and dried,
When the oldest colours have faded, and the youngest critic
   has died,
We shall rest, and, faith, we shall need it – lie down for an
   aeon or two,
Till the Master of all Good Workmen shall put us to work
   anew!

And those that were good shall be happy: they shall sit in a
   golden chair;
They shall splash at a ten-league canvas with brushes of
   comets' hair;
They shall find real saints to draw from – Magdalene, Peter,
   and Paul;
They shall work for an age at a sitting and never be tired at
   all!

And only the Master shall praise us, and only the Master
   shall blame;
And no one shall work for money, and no one shall work
   for fame,
But each for the joy of the working, and each, in his separate
   star,
Shall draw the Thing as he sees It for the God of Things as
   They Are!

The Way Through the Woods

They shut the road through the woods
Seventy years ago.
Weather and rain have undone it again,
And now you would never know

There was once a road through the woods
Before they planted the trees.
It is underneath the coppice and heath
And the thin anemones.
Only the keeper sees
That, where the ring-dove broods,
And the badgers roll at ease,
There was once a road through the woods.

Yet, if you enter the woods
Of a summer evening late,
When the night-air cools on the trout-ringed pools
Where the otter whistles his mate,
(They fear not men in the woods,
Because they see so few)
You will hear the beat of a horse's feet,
And the swish of a skirt in the dew,
Steadily cantering through
The misty solitudes,
As though they perfectly knew
The old lost road through the woods . . .
But there is no road through the woods.

GILBERT MURRAY

(1866–1957)

Born in Sydney, Murray became Professor of Greek at Glasgow University, aged twenty-three. His brilliance and precocity increased, for at forty-two he was Regius Professor of Greek at Oxford. His romantic translations of Euripides' plays into English verse awakened widespread general interest. His own interests extended to many causes: women's rights, vegetarianism and conservative cookery, soft drinks, telepathy, world citizenship and peace. Married to Lady Mary Howard, he counted among his descendants Basil Murray, who died in the Spanish Civil

War, and Philip Toynbee. He was chairman of the League of Nations Union for sixteen years; he was awarded the Order of Merit in 1941. Baptised a Roman Catholic, he lost his faith but found it again at the end.

from: *The Trojan Women*

Troy has been sacked by the Greeks, after a ten-year siege, and the Trojan women, including their queen Hecuba, are enslaved.

Euripides' indignation at the sufferings of war was reflected in Murray's own pity for humanity.

(The day slowly dawns: Hecuba wakes.)

HECUBA   Up from the earth, O weary head!
         This is not Troy, about, above –
         Not Troy, nor we the lords thereof.
     Thou breaking neck, be strengthenèd!

     Endure and chafe not. The winds rave
         And falter. Down the world's wide road,
         Float, float where streams the breath of God;
     Nor turn thy prow to breast the wave.

     Ah woe! . . . For what woe lacketh here?
         My children lost, my land, my lord.
         O thou great wealth of glory, stored
     Of old in Ilion,[1] year by year

     We watched . . . and wert thou nothingness?
         What is there that I fear to say?
         And yet, what help? . . . Ah, well-a-day,
     This ache of lying, comfortless

[1] Troy.

And haunted! Ah, my side, my brow
   And temples! All with changeful pain
   My body rocketh, and would fain:
Move to the tune of ears that flow:
For tears are music too, and keep
A song unheard in hearts that weep.

Cassandra, daughter of Hecuba, a prophetess, sees that the defeated Trojans are less wretched than the conquering Greeks.

CASSANDRA   But we – what pride,
What praise of men were sweeter? – fighting died
To save our people. And when war was red
Around us, friends upbore the gentle dead
Home, and dear women's hands about them wound
White shrouds, and here they sleep in the old ground
Belovèd. And the rest long days fought on,
Dwelling with wives and children, not alone
And joyless, like these Greeks.
              And Hector's[1] woe
What is it? He is gone, and all men know
His glory, and how true a heart he bore.
It is the gift the Greek hath brought!

Wife of Hector, Andromache is to be the slave and concubine of Pyrrhus, son of the Greek hero, Achilles.

ANDROMACHE   One night,
One night . . . aye, men have said it . . . maketh tame
A woman in a man's arms. . . . O shame, shame!
What woman's lips can so forswear her dead,
And give strange kisses in another's bed?
Why, not a dumb beast, not a colt[2] will run
In the yoke untroubled, when her mate is gone –
A thing not in God's image, dull, unmoved
Of reason. . . .

---

[1] A Trojan hero, Hecuba's son.

[2] Murray should perhaps have written mare or filly, since a colt is a young male horse.

*Hecuba mourns her son Hector's child whom the Greeks have hurled to
death from the walls of Troy.*

HECUBA   Dear God, the pattering welcomes of thy feet,
The nursing in my lap; and O, the sweet
Falling asleep together! All is gone.
How should a poet carve the funeral stone
To tell thy story true? 'There lieth here
A babe whom the Greeks feared, and in their fear
Slew him.'

JOHN MASEFIELD

(1878–1967)

*The death of Masefield's mother when he was six abruptly terminated
his blissful Herefordshire childhood. At thirteen he joined the merchant
navy but jumped ship and became a bum in America. He began writing,
and, on returning home, his active literary career opened with the*
Salt-Water Ballads, *a much better way for him to 'go down to the seas
again'. According to Sir John Betjeman, he never gave the impression
of being 'a tweedy, breezy sea-salt' but was skilful at verse-speaking,
with a melodious voice. The title of one of his novels,* Odtaa (One
Damned Thing After Another), *made a minor sensation when published in 1926. He was awarded the Order of Merit in 1935.*

from: SALT-WATER BALLADS

A Consecration

Not the ruler for me, but the ranker, the tramp of the road,
The slave with the sack on his shoulders pricked on with
    the goad,
The man with too weighty a burden, too weary a load.

The sailor, the stoker of steamers, the man with the clout,
The chantryman bent at the halliards putting a tune to the
    shout,
The drowsy man at the wheel and the tired look-out.

Others may sing of the wine and the wealth and the mirth,
The portly presence of potentates goodly in girth; –
Mine be the dirt and the dross, the dust and scum of the
    earth!

Theirs be the music, the colour, the glory, the gold;
Mine be a handful of ashes, a mouthful of mould,
Of the maimed, of the halt and the blind in the rain and the
    cold –

Of these shall my songs be fashioned, my tales be told.

AMEN

Sea-Fever

I must go down to the seas again, to the lonely sea and the
    sky,
And all I ask is a tall ship and a star to steer her by,
And the wheel's kick and wind's song and the white sail's
    shaking,
And a grey mist on the sea's face and a grey dawn breaking.

I must go down to the seas again, for the call of the running
    tide
Is a wild call and clear call that may not be denied;
And all I ask is a windy day with the white clouds flying,
And the flung spray and the blown spume, and the sea-gulls
    crying.

I must go down to the seas again, to the vagrant gypsy life,
To the gull's way and the whale's way where the wind's like
  a whetted knife;
And all I ask is a merry yarn from a laughing fellow-rover,
And quiet sleep and a sweet dream when the long trick's
  over.

Cargoes

Quinquireme of Nineveh from distant Ophir
Rowing home to haven in sunny Palestine,
With a cargo of ivory,
And apes and peacocks,
Sandalwood, cedarwood, and sweet white wine.

Stately Spanish galleon coming from the Isthmus,
Dipping through the Tropics by the palm-green shores,
With a cargo of diamonds,
Emeralds, amethysts,
Topazes, and cinnamon, and gold moidores.

Dirty British coaster with a salt-caked smoke stack
Butting through the channel in the mad March days,
With a cargo of Tyne coal,
Road-rail, pig-lead,
Firewood, iron-ware, and cheap tin trays.

from: *Pompey the Great*
ACT I

The Centurion speaks.

Man is a sacred city, built of marvellous earth,
Life was lived nobly here to give this body birth.[1]

---

[1] Another version of the first two lines of this poem is found in the anthology *Poems of To-day*,
which I personally prefer:

> This was a sacred city, built of marvellous earth,
> Life was lived nobly here to give such beauty birth.

Something was in this brain and in this eager hand.
Death is so dumb and blind, Death cannot understand.
. Death drifts the brain with dust and soils the young limbs'
  glory.
Death makes women a dream and men a traveller's story.
Death drives the lovely soul to wander under the sky,
Death opens unknown doors. It is most grand to die.

 # DAVID HERBERT LAWRENCE

(1885–1930)

D. H. Lawrence was the son of a Nottinghamshire miner. As well as teaching, he worked briefly in a surgical goods factory – about as appropriate to his passionate temperament as Guy's Hospital was to Keats's. His first great novel, Sons and Lovers, *described the unhappy marriage of his adored mother and detested father. He eloped with an older married woman, Frieda, née von Richthofen. Their subsequent marriage was no more harmonious than his parents'. He wandered with Frieda – but without enough money – over Europe, America and Mexico. His writings sought to bring to light and inflame the 'dark' forces of nature, especially sex, much as his father had dragged out coal. He was often prophetic, sometimes silly, never obscene, always vital. He died of tuberculosis.*

From a letter to Lady Cynthia Asquith, written in Hampstead, 28 November 1915.

> Now like a crocus in the autumn time,
> My soul comes naked from the falling night
> Of death, a Cyclamen, a Crocus flower
> Of windy autumn when the winds all sweep
> The hosts away to death, where heap on heap
> The leaves are smouldering in a funeral wind.

For God's Sake –

From a letter to Charles Wilson, written in Var, France, 28 December 1928.

For God's sake, let us be men,
not monkeys minding machines,
or sitting with our tails curled
while the machine amuses us, radio or film or gramophone.
Monkeys with a bland grin on our faces.

O! Start a Revolution!

O! start a revolution, somebody!
not to get the money
but to lose it all for ever.

O! start a revolution, somebody!
not to install the working classes
but to abolish the working classes for ever
and leave a world of men.

It's Either You Fight or You Die

It's either you fight or you die,
young gents, you've got no option.
No good asking the reason why.
It's either you fight or you die,
die, die, lily-liveredly die,
or fight and make the splinters fly,
bust up the holy apple pie,
you've got no option.

Don't say you can't, start in and try,
give nice hypocrisy the lie,
and tackle the blowsy, big blow-fly
of money; do it or die,
you've got no option.

THOMAS STEARNS ELIOT

(1888–1965)

T. S. or Tom Eliot, as he was known, was born in the United States and emigrated to England early in the Great War, joining Lloyds Bank as a clerk. His first unhappy marriage began at about the same time and lasted until his disturbed wife died in 1947. Meanwhile Eliot had become a director of Faber's publishing house and a major influence on modern poetry: a social traditionalist if ever there was one, but a radical innovator in poetic form and a powerful if conservative literary critic; an Anglo-Catholic who could express religious doubt equally with mysticism. Personally, I found him quiet, simple and friendly, without any signs of the pervading irony, parody and echo that stamped his poetry. His second wife, Valerie, has contributed both to his later happiness and to the understanding of his writings.

from: *Choruses from 'The Rock'*

The Eagle soars in the summit of Heaven,
The Hunter with his dogs pursues his circuit.
O perpetual revolution of configured stars,
O perpetual recurrence of determined seasons,
O world of spring and autumn, birth and dying!
The endless cycle of idea and action,
Endless invention, endless experiment,
Brings knowledge of motion, but not of stillness;
Knowledge of speech, but not of silence;
Knowledge of words, and ignorance of the Word.
All our knowledge brings us nearer to our ignorance,
All our ignorance brings us nearer to death,
But nearness to death no nearer to GOD.
Where is the Life we have lost in living?
Where is the wisdom we have lost in knowledge?
Where is the knowledge we have lost in information?
The cycles of Heaven in twenty centuries
Bring us farther from GOD and nearer to the Dust.

I journeyed to London, to the timekept City,
Where the River flows, with foreign flotations.
There I was told: we have too many churches,
And too few chop-houses. There I was told:
Let the vicars retire. Men do not need the Church
In the place where they work, but where they spend their
    Sundays.
In the City, we need no bells:
Let them waken the suburbs.
I journeyed to the suburbs and there I was told:
We toil for six days, on the seventh we must motor
To Hindhead, or Maidenhead.
If the weather is foul we stay at home and read the papers.
In industrial districts, there I was told
Of economic laws.
In the pleasant countryside, there it seemed
That the country now is only fit for picnics,
And the Church does not seem to be wanted
In country or in suburbs; and in the town
Only for important weddings.

from: FIVE-FINGER EXERCISES

II. Lines to a Yorkshire Terrier

*Notice the echoes in the last six lines of Edward Lear, Shakespeare and
'Grace before Meat' by Herrick.*

In a brown field stood a tree
And the tree was crookt and dry.
In a black sky, from a green cloud
Natural forces shriek'd aloud,
Screamed, rattled, muttered endlessly.
Little dog was safe and warm
Under a cretonne eiderdown,
Yet the field was cracked and brown
And the tree was cramped and dry.

Pollicle dogs and cats all must
Jellicle cats and dogs all must
Like undertakers, come to dust.
Here a little dog I pause
Heaving up my prior paws,
Pause, and sleep endlessly.

WYSTAN HUGH AUDEN

(1907–1973)

Son of a Birmingham medical officer of health, Auden went to a Quaker school and then to Oxford, where he met Louis MacNeice and Stephen Spender, all three to be 'Pylon Poets' because of their interest in pylons and gasworks rather than 'poetic' subjects. Auden at first saw salvation through the socialist state, eloquently backing the Republicans in the Spanish Civil War. Though a homosexual, he married a Jewish girl, the daughter of Thomas Mann, to rescue her from Nazi Germany. Before the Second World War he began to see salvation through the individual love of God and neighbour – Christianity. He left England to live in America and took American citizenship. At forty-nine he returned to Oxford as Professor of Poetry, living there and at his home in Austria until his death.

from: *Spain – April 1937*

Later Auden disowned this unforgettable poem as 'trash'.

Yesterday all the past. The language of size
Spreading to China along the trade-routes; the diffusion
     Of the counting-frame and the cromlech;
Yesterday the shadow-reckoning in the sunny climates. . . .

The trial of heretics among the columns of stone;
Yesterday the theological feuds in the taverns
     And the miraculous cure at the fountain;
Yesterday the Sabbath of witches; but to-day the
     struggle. . . .

*The poet, the medical researcher, the astronomer, the poor send up their
cries.*

And the nations combine each cry, invoking the life
That shapes the individual belly and orders
    The private nocturnal terror;
'Did you not found the city state of the sponge,

'Raise the vast military empires of the shark
And the tiger, establish the robin's plucky canton?
    Intervene. O descend as a dove or
A furious papa or a mild engineer, but descend.' . . .

*'The life' replies that today it is not 'the mover', simply their own
actions.*

'What's your proposal? To build the just city? I will.
I agree. Or is it the suicide pact, the romantic
    Death? Very well, I accept, for
I am your choice, your decision. Yes, I am Spain.' . . .

To-morrow, perhaps the future. The research on fatigue
And the movements of packers; the gradual exploring
    of all the
    Octaves of radiation;
To-morrow the enlarging of consciousness by diet and
    breathing.

To-morrow the rediscovery of romantic love,
The photographing of ravens; all the fun under
    Liberty's masterful shadow;
To-morrow the hour of the pageant-master and the
    musician,

The beautiful roar of the chorus under the dome;
To-morrow the exchanging of tips on the breeding of
    terriers,
    The eager election of chairmen
By the sudden forest of hands. But to-day the struggle.

from: *At the Grave of Henry James*

c. Spring 1941.

All will be judged. Master of nuance and scruple,
Pray for me and for all writers living or dead:
  Because there are many whose works
Are in better taste than their lives;
  because there is no end
To the vanity of our calling: make intercession
  For the treason of all clerks.

Because the darkness is never so distant,
And there is never much time for the arrogant
  Spirit to flutter its wings,
Or the broken bone to rejoice, or the cruel to cry
For Him whose property is always to have mercy, the author
  And giver of all good things.

from: *The Sea and the Mirror*

A Commentary on Shakespeare's The Tempest *1942–1944*

III CALIBAN TO THE AUDIENCE

Yet, at this very moment when we do at last see ourselves as we
are, neither cosy nor playful, but swaying out on the ultimate
wind-whipped cornice that overhangs the unabiding void – we
have never stood anywhere else, . . . it is at this moment that for
the first time in our lives we hear, not the sounds which, as
born actors, we have hitherto condescended to use as an excellent
vehicle for displaying our personalities and looks, but the real
Word which is our only *raison d'être*.

DYLAN THOMAS

(1914–1953)

Born in Swansea and educated at the grammar school – his father was the English master – Thomas wrote and spoke only English, though profoundly influenced by Wales and the Welsh. He wrote poetry at school and became a London journalist, broadcaster and convivial drinker, until he married and lived for a time in the romantically situated Welsh village of Laugharne, which he made famous. His natural ebullience revelled in but eventually succumbed to American lecture-tours; the candle, burnt at both ends, went out during the fourth. Thomas brought back to English poetry something of the 'Mermaid Tavern' tradition, appearing more of a Marlowe than anything that had been seen for centuries. He has a fine following among his own and the next generations.

Do Not Go Gentle into that Good Night

For his father.

> Do not go gentle into that good night,
> Old age should burn and rave at close of day;
> Rage, rage against the dying of the light.
>
> Though wise men at their end know dark is right,
> Because their words had forked no lightning they
> Do not go gentle into that good night.
>
> Good men, the last wave by, crying how bright
> Their frail deeds might have danced in a green bay,
> Rage, rage against the dying of the light.
>
> Wild men who caught and sang the sun in flight,
> And learn, too late, they grieved it on its way,
> Do not go gentle into that good night.

Grave men, near death, who see with blinding sight
Blind eyes could blaze like meteors and be gay,
Rage, rage against the dying of the light.

And you, my father, there on the sad height,
Curse, bless me now with your fierce tears, I pray.
Do not go gentle into that good night,
Rage, rage against the dying of the light.

from: *Under Milk Wood*

POLLY GARTER'S SONG

FIRST VOICE: The morning is all singing. The Reverend Eli
Jenkins, busy on his morning calls, stops outside the Welfare
Hall to hear Polly Garter as she scrubs the floors for the
Mothers' Union Dance to-night.

POLLY GARTER   I loved a man whose name was Tom
[Singing]   He was strong as a bear and two yards long
I loved a man whose name was Dick
He was big as a barrel and three feet thick
And I loved a man whose name was Harry
Six feet tall and sweet as a cherry
But the one I loved best awake or asleep
Was little Willy Wee and he's six feet deep.

O Tom Dick and Harry were three fine men
And I'll never have such loving again
But little Willy Wee who took me on his knee
Little Willy Wee was the man for me.

Now men from every parish round
Run after me and roll me on the ground
But whenever I love another man back
Johnnie from the Hill or sailing Jack
I always think as they do what they please
Of Tom Dick and Harry who were tall as trees
And most I think when I'm by their side
Of little Willy Wee who drowned and died.

O Tom Dick and Harry were three fine men
And I'll never have such loving again
But little Willy Wee who took me on his knee
Little Willy Weazel was the man for me.

REVD ELI   Praise the Lord! We are a musical nation.
JENKINS

SECOND VOICE And the Reverend Jenkins hurries on through the
town to visit the sick with jelly and poems. . . .

ELI JENKINS'S SUNSET POEM

FIRST VOICE And at the door of Bethesda House, the Reverend
Jenkins recites to Llareggub Hill his sunset poem.

REVD ELI   Every morning when I wake,
JENKINS   Dear Lord, a little prayer I make,
            O please to keep thy lovely eye
            On all poor creatures born to die.

            And every evening at sundown
            I ask a blessing on the town,
            For whether we last the night or no
            I'm sure is always touch-and-go.

We are not wholly bad or good
Who live our lives under Milk Wood,
And Thou, I know, wilt be the first
To see our best side, not our worst.

O let us see another day!
Bless us all this night, I pray,
And to the sun we all will bow
And say, good-bye – but just for now!

THE FIRST WORLD WAR POETS

Out of the sixteen poets commemorated together in Poets' Corner, six were killed in the war. But the division between the dead and the survivors is not the one to look out for when reading their poetry.

The real difference comes between those who were exalted by the 'glory' and patriotic sacrifice of war, and those who were overwhelmed by its pity and horror. It will be found that Brooke and Grenfell were the clearest examples of the first type. Grenfell wrote: 'And he is dead who will not fight' – reminding us of the King's speech before the battle of Agincourt, in Shakespeare's Henry V:

> 'And gentlemen in England now abed
> Shall think themselves accursed they were not here.'

Striking examples of the opposite type were Read and Sassoon. In between we can perhaps place the poets who changed during the war itself from heroic idealism to anger and bitterness. Binyon and Owen showed how this could happen. Owen came to dislike his sonnet, 'Anthem for Doomed Youth', because of what he saw as its sentimentality. Others may still see in it genuine pity expressed in true poetry.

The change in emphasis from 'glory' to 'mud and blood' occurred after 1916 with the battle of the Somme. Brooke and Grenfell died in 1915.

Two inspirations for many of these war poets will be found in the English countryside and in the comrades, the 'men'.

The epitaph on the memorial stone in Poets' Corner was taken from Owen's lines:

> My subject is War, and the pity of War.
> The Poetry is in the pity.

RICHARD ALDINGTON

(1892–1962)

A 'trench poet', Aldington expressed his experiences of the war also in a novel, Death of a Hero, *first published in expurgated form. He was interested in aesthetics and became an Imagist before the war, like his American friends Ezra Pound and 'H. D.' (Hilda Doolittle), whom he married. Introducing a collected edition of his poems (1929), Aldington wrote that the aim of himself and his friends was to rescue poetry from Romanticism and Victorianism. One method was to keep poems short, and about objects. 'We were fearfully intolerant . . .' Later he exchanged letters with Lawrence Durrell, published in 1981.*

from: IMAGES OF WAR

In the Trenches

I

Not that we are weary,
Not that we fear,
Not that we are lonely
Though never alone –
Not these, not these destroy us;
But that each rush and crash
Of mortar and shell,
Each cruel bitter shriek of bullet
That tears the wind like a blade,
Each wound on the breast of earth,
Of Demeter, our Mother,
Wound us also,
Sever and rend the fine fabric
Of the wings of our frail souls,
Scatter into dust the bright wings
Of Psyche!

Impotent,
How impotent is all this clamour,
This destruction and contest . . .

Night after night comes the moon
Haughty and perfect;
Night after night the Pleiades sing
And Orion swings his belt across the sky.
Night after night the frost
Crumbles the hard earth.

Soon the spring will drop flowers
And patient creeping stalk and leaf
Along these barren lines
Where the huge rats scuttle
And the hawk shrieks to the carrion crow.

Can you stay them with your noise?
Then kill winter with your cannon,
Hold back Orion with your bayonets,
And crush the spring leaf with your armies!

Battlefield

The wind is piercing chill
And blows fine grains of snow
Over this shell-rent ground;
Every house in sight
Is smashed and desolate.

But in this fruitless land,
Thorny with wire
And foul with rotting clothes and sacks,
The crosses flourish –
Ci-gît, ci-gît, ci-gît . . .
'Ci-gît 1 soldat Allemand,
Priez pour lui.'

LAURENCE BINYON

(1869–1943)

Born in Lancaster, son of a vicar, Binyon came of Quaker stock on both sides. After a brilliant career at Oxford (he won the Newdigate), Binyon entered the department of prints and drawings at the British Museum, becoming keeper of the newly formed oriental department of the same. He combined poetic with visual gifts, especially in his knowledge of oriental art. He served in the war as a Red Cross orderly, being created a chevalier of the French Legion of Honour, and Companion of Honour in 1932. In his poetry he was influenced by the rhythmic innovations of Robert Bridges and Gerard Manley Hopkins. The haunting appeal of 'For the Fallen' lies partly in its natural 'stress accent'.

The Little Dancers

Lonely, save for a few faint stars, the sky
Dreams; and lonely, below, the little street
Into its gloom retires, secluded and shy.
Scarcely the dumb roar enters this soft retreat;
And all is dark, save where come flooding rays
From a tavern-window; there, to the brisk measure
Of an organ that down in an alley merrily plays,
Two children, all alone and no one by,
Holding their tattered frocks, thro' an airy maze
Of motion lightly threaded with nimble feet
Dance sedately; face to face they gaze,
Their eyes shining, grave with a perfect pleasure.

from: *For the Fallen*

Published in The Times, *21 September 1914.*

With proud thanksgiving, a mother for her children,
England mourns for her dead across the sea.
Flesh of her flesh they were, spirit of her spirit,
Fallen in the cause of the free.

Solemn the drums thrill: Death august and royal
Sings sorrow up into immortal spheres.
There is music in the midst of desolation
And a glory that shines upon our tears.

They went with songs to the battle, they were young,
Straight of limb, true of eye, steady and aglow.
They were staunch to the end against odds uncounted,
They fell with their faces to the foe.

They shall grow not old, as we that are left grow old:
Age shall not weary them, nor the years condemn.
At the going down of the sun and in the morning
We will remember them. . . .

As the stars that shall be bright when we are dust
Moving in marches upon the heavenly plain,
As the stars that are starry in the time of our darkness,
To the end, to the end, they remain.

from: *Oxford in Wartime*

What alters you, familiar lawn and tower,
Arched alley, and garden green to the grey wall
With crumbling crevice and the old wine-red flower,
Solitary in summer sun? for all

Is like a dream: I tread on dreams! No stir
Of footsteps, voices, laughter! Even the chime
Of many-memoried bells is lonelier
In this neglected ghostliness of Time. ...

It is as if I looked on the still face
Of a Mother, musing where she sits alone.
She is with her sons, she is not like this place;
She is gone out into far lands unknown. ...

She is with her sons, leaving a virtue gone
Out of her sacred places: what she bred
Lives other life than this, that sits alone,
Though still in dream starrily visited!

EDMUND BLUNDEN

(1896–1974)

*Poet, critic, biographer, teacher, Blunden lived longer than most of the
War Poets and used many of those extra years in publicising the dead:
Owen and Gurney. Born in London, his home and inspiration became
Kent and its countryside. A 'trench poet' from 1914 on, his experiences
of the war were fused with and affected all the rest of a full life. Even
when he was living in Oxford in the 1940s, his sensitive diffidence
seemed more of a haunting than a case of poetic temperament. He had
been appointed professor in Hong Kong after teaching in Tokyo. In 1966
he was elected Professor of Poetry at Oxford.*

Vlamertinghe: Passing the Château, July 1917

*The poet is thinking of the sacrificial procession in Keats's 'Ode on a
Grecian Urn' in relation to Flanders' fields.*

'And all her silken flanks with garlands drest' –
But we are coming to a sacrifice.
Must those have flowers who are not yet gone West?
May those have flowers who live with death and lice?
This must be the floweriest place
That earth allows; the queenly face
Of the proud mansion borrows grace for grace
Spite of those brute guns lowing at the skies.

Bold great daisies' golden lights,
Bubbling roses' pinks and whites –
Such a gay carpet! poppies by the million;
Such damask! such vermilion!
But if you ask me, mate, the choice of colour
Is scarcely right; this red should have been duller.

The Waggoner, 1919

The old waggon drudges through the miry lane,
    By the skulking pond where the pollards frown,
Notched dumb surly images of pain;
    On a dulled earth the night droops down.

Wincing to slow and wistful airs
    The leaves on the shrubbed oaks know their hour,
And the unknown wandering spoiler bares
    The thorned black hedge of a mournful shower.

Small bodies fluster in the dead brown wrack
    As the stumbling shaft-horse jingles past
And the waggoner flicks his whip a crack;
    The odd light flares on shadows vast

Over the lodges and oasts and byres
    Of the darkened farm; the moment hangs wan
As though nature flagged and all desires.
    But in the dim court the ghost is gone

From the hug-secret yew to the penthouse wall
  And stooping there seems to listen to
The waggoner leading the gray to stall,
  As centuries past itself would do.

from: *1916 seen from 1921*

Tired with dull grief, grown old before my day,
I sit in solitude and only hear
Long silent laughters, murmurings of dismay,
The lost intensities of hope and fear;
In those old marshes yet the rifles lie,
On the thin breastwork flutter the grey rags,
The very books I read are there – and I
Dead as the men I loved, wait while life drags

Its wounded length from those sad streets of war
Into green places here, that were my own;
But now what once was mine is mine no more,
I seek such neighbours here and I find none.
With such strong gentleness and tireless will
Those ruined houses seared themselves in me,
Passionate I look for their dumb story still,
And the charred stub outspeaks the living tree.

RUPERT BROOKE

(1887–1915)

Son of a schoolmaster at Rugby where he was born, Brooke presented the perfect picture of a dazzling young poet: a romantic friend, a writer of verses with an idealistic appeal that was within everyone's reach, a sensuous love of the natural world. Educated at King's, Cambridge and living afterwards nearby at Grantchester, he remembered the lyrical life there when on his travels:

Stands the Church clock at ten to three?
And is there honey still for tea?

He died at Skyros of septicaemia in April 1915, a touching example of the unclouded patriotism that inspired the early years of the Great War. He seemed to be summed up in Frances Cornford's epigram:

A young Apollo, golden-haired,
　　Stands dreaming on the verge of strife,
Magnificently unprepared
　　For the long littleness of life.

However, his friend and editor, Eddie Marsh, suggested after his death that 'long littleness' must now read 'brief greatness'.

from: 1914

These five sonnets Rupert Brooke called his 'five camp-children'. '4 and 5 are good though, and there are phrases in the rest.'

IV. THE DEAD

These hearts were woven of human joys and cares,
　　Washed marvellously with sorrow, swift to mirth.
The years had given them kindness. Dawn was theirs,
　　And sunset, and the colours of the earth.
These had seen movement, and heard music; known
　　Slumber and waking; loved; gone proudly friended;
Felt the quick stir of wonder; sat alone;
　　Touched flowers and furs and cheeks. All this is ended.

There are waters blown by changing winds to laughter
And lit by the rich skies, all day. And after,
　　Frost, with a gesture, stays the waves that dance
And wandering loveliness. He leaves a white
　　Unbroken glory, a gathered radiance,
A width, a shining peace, under the night.

If I should die, think only this of me:
　That there's some corner of a foreign field
That is for ever England. There shall be
　In that rich earth a richer dust concealed;
A dust whom England bore, shaped, made aware,
　Gave, once, her flowers to love, her ways to roam,
A body of England's, breathing English air,
　Washed by the rivers, blest by suns of home.

And think, this heart, all evil shed away,
　A pulse in the eternal mind, no less
　　Gives somewhere back the thoughts by England given;
Her sights and sounds; dreams happy as her day;
　And laughter, learnt of friends; and gentleness,
　　In hearts at peace, under an English heaven.

from: *Menelaus and Helen*

In the first of these two sonnets, King Menelaus has won the ten-year Trojan War, revenged himself on Paris who ran off with Helen, his wife, and intends to slay her also – but her magical beauty subdues him once again.

II

So far the poet. How should he behold
　That journey home, the long connubial years?
　He does not tell you how white Helen bears
Child on legitimate child, becomes a scold,
Haggard with virtue. Menelaus bold
　Waxed garrulous, and sacked a hundred Troys
　'Twixt noon and supper. And her golden voice
Got shrill as he grew deafer. And both were old.

Often he wonders why on earth he went
    Troyward, or why poor Paris ever came.
Oft she weeps, gummy-eyed and impotent;
    Her dry shanks twitch at Paris' mumbled name.
So Menelaus nagged; and Helen cried;
And Paris slept on by Scamander side.

WILFRID GIBSON

(1878–1962)

*Born in Northumberland, Gibson became a published poet in his twenties
and a Londoner at thirty-four. He contributed to* Georgian Poetry
*(George V), founded in 1912 by his friends Eddie Marsh and Rupert
Brooke among others. He shared much of Brooke's romanticism about
the war and was appointed one of Brooke's heirs when he died on active
service in 1915. Gibson's 'Lament' was almost as popular as Brooke's
'The Dead' and Binyon's 'For the Fallen'. But as one of the war's
survivors, Gibson wrote poems from 1916 onwards that began to show
signs of the future realism.*

from: FRIENDS (1916)

To the Memory of Rupert Brooke, 23 April 1915

He's gone.
I do not understand:
I only know
That as he turned to go
And waved his hand
In his young eyes a sudden glory shone,
And I was dazzled by a sunset glow,
And he was gone.

Rupert Brooke II

Once in my garret – you being far away
Tramping the hills, and breathing upland air,
Or so I fancied – brooding in my chair,
I watched the London sunlight feeble and grey
Dapple my desk, too tired to labour more,
When, looking up, I saw you standing there,
Although I'd caught no footstep on the stair,
Like a sudden April at my open door.

Though now beyond earth's farthest hills you fare,
Song-crowned, immortal, sometimes it seems to me
That if I listen very quietly
Perhaps I'll hear your footstep on the stair
And see you, standing with your angel air,
Fresh from the uplands of eternity.

from: BATTLE

Breakfast

We ate our breakfast lying on our backs
Because the shells were screeching overhead.
I bet a rasher to a loaf of bread
That Hull United would beat Halifax
When Jimmy Stainthorpe played full-back instead
Of Billy Bradford. Ginger raised his head
And cursed, and took the bet, and dropt back dead.
We ate our breakfast lying on our backs
Because the shells were screeching overhead.

Mark Anderson

On the low table by the bed
Where it[1] was set aside last night,
Beyond the bandaged lifeless head,
It glitters in the morning light.

And as the hours of morning pass
I cannot sleep, I cannot think,
But only gaze upon the glass
Of water that he could not drink.

Lament

We who are left, how shall we look again
Happily on the sun or feel the rain,
Without remembering how they who went
Ungrudgingly, and spent
Their all for us, loved too the sun and rain?

A bird among the rain-wet lilac sings –
But we, how shall we turn to little things,
And listen to the birds and winds and streams
Made holy by their dreams,
Nor feel the heart-break in the heart of things?

ROBERT GRAVES

(1895–1985)

Son of a Dublin school inspector but born and brought up in England,
Graves joined the army in 1914. Though his first war poems were
published in 1916, he had suppressed them all by 1927, except for
'Armistice Day'. It was indeed, like the title of his famous autobiography,

---

[1] The glass.

Goodbye to All That *(1929)*. *War poems were 'a fashion', he said, many written by civilians. His prolific post-war writings included poetry and historical fiction* (I, Claudius). *He married twice and lived for twelve years with the distinguished American poet, Laura Riding (1901–1991).*

from: To Lucasta On Going to the Wars – For the Fourth Time

This poem combines regimental pride with scepticism.

> It doesn't matter what's the cause,
>   What wrong they say we're righting,
> A curse for treaties, bonds and laws,
>   When we've to do the fighting!
> And since we lads are proud and true,
>   What else remains to do?
> Lucasta, when to France your man
> Returns his fourth time, hating war,
> Yet laughs as calmly as he can
>   And flings an oath, but says no more,
> That is not courage, that's not fear –
> Lucasta he's a Fusilier,
>   And his pride sends him here.

from: Familiar Letters to Siegfried Sassoon
FROM BIVOUACS AT MAMETZ WOOD, JULY 13TH 1916

Graves's idyllic, ironical plans for 'after the war'.

> In Gweithdy Bach we'll rest a while,
> We'll dress our wounds and learn to smile
> With easier lips; we'll stretch our legs,
> And live on bilberry tart and eggs,
> And store up solar energy,
> Basking in sunshine by the sea,

Until we feel a match once more
For *anything* but another war.
So then we'll kiss our families,
And sail away across the seas
(The God of Song protecting us)
To the great hills of Caucasus.

from: *Armistice Day, 1918*

What's all this hubbub and yelling,
    Commotion and scamper of feet,
With ear-splitting clatter of kettles and cans,
    Wild laughter down Mafeking Street?

O, those are the kids whom we fought for
    (You might think they'd been scoffing our rum)
With flags that they waved when we marched off to war
    In the rapture of bugle and drum.

Now they'll hang Kaiser Bill from a lamp-post,
    Von Tirpitz they'll hang from a tree . . .
We've been promised a 'Land Fit for Heroes' –
    What heroes we heroes must be! . . .

But there's old men and women in corners
    With tears falling fast on their cheeks,
There's the armless and legless and sightless –
    It's seldom that one of them speaks. . . .

When the days of rejoicing are over,
    When the flags are stowed safely away,
They will dream of another wild 'War to end Wars'
    And another wild Armistice Day.

But the boys who were killed in the trenches,
    Who fought with no rage and no rant,
We left them stretched out on their pallets of mud
    Low down with the worm and the ant.

Graves's cynicism about the war and himself was also reflected in two lines parodying Rupert Brooke. Graves was a long-term survivor, living to be ninety.

> When I'm killed, don't think of me
> Buried there in Cambrin Wood.

JULIAN GRENFELL

(1888–1915)

Born into the aristocratic Desborough family, Grenfell was brought up by his aspiring mother – she was one of the Souls – to regard himself as a god among mortals. His career at Eton and Balliol added to his glamour. A champion boxer, at twenty-two he joined the regular army and went to fight in 1914 as a member of the generation that is sometimes called 'lost', sometimes 'golden'. It has been suggested that they had a death wish. Whether or not that was so – and the 'lost generation' all saw themselves as life-enhancers – they had little in common with the later war-time 'generation' of sceptical realists. Julian Grenfell, DSO died of wounds at Ypres.

Into Battle

> The naked earth is warm with Spring,
>   And with green grass and bursting trees
> Leans to the sun's gaze glorying,
>   And quivers in the sunny breeze;
> And Life is Colour and Warmth and Light,
>   And a striving evermore for these;
> And he is dead who will not fight,
>   And who dies fighting has increase.

The fighting man shall from the sun
  Take warmth, and life from the glowing earth;
Speed with the light-foot winds to run,
  And with the trees to newer birth;
And find, when fighting shall be done,
  Great rest, and fullness after dearth.

All the bright company of heaven
  Hold him in their high comradeship,
The Dog-Star, and the Sisters Seven,
  Orion's belt and sworded hip.

The woodland trees that stand together,
  They stand to him each one a friend;
They gently speak in the windy weather;
  They guide to valley and ridge's end.

The kestrel hovering by day,
  And the little owls that call by night,
Bid him be swift and keen as they,
  As keen of ear, as swift of sight.

The blackbird sings to him, 'Brother, brother,
  If this be the last song you shall sing,
Sing well, for you may not sing another;
  Brother, sing.'

In dreary, doubtful, waiting hours,
  Before the brazen frenzy starts,
The horses show him nobler powers;
  O patient eyes, courageous hearts!

And when the burning moment breaks,
  And all things else are out of mind,
And only joy of battle takes
  Him by the throat, and makes him blind,

Through joy and blindness he shall know,
  Not caring much to know, that still
Nor lead nor steel shall reach him, so
  That it be not the Destined Will.

The thundering line of battle stands,
  And in the air death moans and sings;
But Day shall clasp him with strong hands,
  And Night shall fold him in soft wings.

IVOR GURNEY

(1890–1937)

Son of a tailor of Gloucester, where he was born, this poet/musician loved winds and trees and country sights as much as any Beatrix Potter. But the war carried Private Gurney to France as a volunteer in 1915, away from his beloved Cotswolds. He suffered all the horrors of the Western Front – wounded, gassed – except death. He was carried away again, even more tragically, in 1922, and died of TB after fifteen years in mental hospitals. His poetry is individual and revealing, his songs original.

Servitude

If it were not for England, who would bear
This heavy servitude one moment more?
To keep a brothel, sweep and wash the floor
Of filthiest hovels were noble to compare
With this brass-cleaning life. Now here, now there
Harried in foolishness, scanned curiously o'er
By fools made brazen by conceit, and store
Of antique witticisms thin and bare.

Only the love of comrades sweetens all,
Whose laughing spirit will not be outdone.
As night-watching men wait for the sun
To hearten them, so wait I on such boys
As neither brass nor Hell-fire may appal,
Nor guns, nor sergeant-major's bluster and noise.

Walking Song

The miles go sliding by
Under my steady feet,
That mark a leisurely
And still unbroken beat,
Through coppices that hear
Awhile, then lie as still
As though no traveller
Ever had climbed their hill.

My comrades are the small
Or dumb or singing birds,
Squirrels, field-things all
And placid drowsing herds.
Companions that I must
Greet for a while, then leave
Scattering the forward dust
From dawn to late of eve.

To God

Why have you made life so intolerable
And set me between four walls, where I am able
Not to escape meals without prayer, for that's possible
Only by annoying an attendant. And tonight a sensual Hell
Has been put on me, so that all has deserted me
And I am merely crying and trembling in heart
For death, and cannot get it. And gone out is part
Of sanity. And there is dreadful hell within me.

And nothing helps. Forced meals there have been and
    electricity
And weakening of sanity by influence
That's dreadful to endure. . . .
Gone out every bright thing from my mind
All lost that ever God himself designed.
Not half can be written of cruelty of man, on man,
Not often such evil guessed as between man and man.

The Songs I Had

The songs I had are withered
Or vanished clean,
Yet there are bright tracks
Where I have been

And there grow flowers
For others' delight.
Think well, O singer,
Soon comes night.

DAVID JONES

(1895–1974)

*Artist and poet, Jones was born in Kent, son of a Welshman. At twenty-
six he joined the Roman Catholic Church, a life-long inspiration, as was
his service as a Welsh infantryman on the Western Front. Feeling as
he did that modern man was being forced by his own technology to live
in a 'megalopolitan twilight', Jones was a dedicated poet: dedicated to
lifting a corner of the veil just as the cross is unveiled bit by bit on
Good Friday. He drew a number of his symbols from Celtic culture.
In Parenthesis shows his comrades in the Royal Welch Fusiliers as
torch-bearers of that culture and war's sacred victims. He received the
Companion of Honour in 1974.*

from: *In Parenthesis*

PART 7

Private John Ball is the hero of this prose-poetry. They are told to dig in, and the next man to Ball is hit as he digs.

The first Field Dressing is futile as frantic seaman's shift
bunged to stoved bulwark, so soon the darking flood
percolates and he dies in your arms.
    And get back to that digging can't yer –
this ain't a bloody Wake
      for these dead, who soon will have their dead
for burial clods heaped over.
Nor time for halsing[1]
nor to clip green wounds
nor weeping Maries bringing anointments
neither any word spoken
nor no decent nor appropriate sowing of this seed
nor remembrance of the harvesting
of the renascent cycle
and return
nor shaving of the head nor ritual incising for these
viriles under each tree.
    No one sings: Lully lully
for the mate whose blood runs down.
Corposant his signal flare[2]
      makes its slow parabola
where acorn hanging cross-trees tangle
and the leafy tops intersect.
And white faces lie,
(like china saucers tilted run soiling stains half dry, when
    the moon shines on a scullery-rack and Mr and Mrs
    Billington are asleep upstairs and so's Vi – and any creak
    frightens you or any twig moving.)

And it's nearing dark when the trench is digged and they
brought forward R.E.s who methodically spaced their

---

[1] Auguring.   [2] St Elmo's fire.

picket-irons and did their work back and fro, speak low –
cats-cradle tenuous gear.
You can hear their mauls[1]
under the oaks.

And when they've done the job they file back carrying
their implements, and the covering Lewis team withdraws
from out in front and the water-party is up at last with half
the bottles punctured
and travellers' tales.
Stammer a tale stare-eyed of close shaves,
of outside on the open slope:
Carrying-parties,
runners who hasten singly,
burdened bearers walk with careful feet
to jolt him as little as possible,
bearers of burdens to and from
stumble oftener, notice the lessening light,
and feel their way with more sensitive feet –
you musn't spill the precious fragments, for perhaps these
raw bones live.

They can cover him again with skin – in their candid[2]
coats,
in their clinical shrines and parade the miraculi.[3]

The blinded one with the artificial guts – his morbid
neurosis
retards the treatment, otherwise he's bonza – and will learn
a handicraft.

Nothing is impossible nowadays my dear if only we can get
the poor bleeder through the barrage and they take just
as much trouble with the ordinary soldiers you know and
essential-service academicians can match the natural hue
and everything extraordinarily well.

Give them glass eyes to see
and synthetic spare parts to walk in the Triumphs, without
anyone feeling awkward and O, O, O, it's a lovely war
with poppies on the up-platform.

[1] Mallets.   [2] White.   [3] Considered miraculous.

—{ 212 }—

ROBERT NICHOLS

(1893–1944)

Born in the Isle of Wight and educated at Winchester and Oxford, Nichols came of a family that included a poet (his father), an ambassador (brother) and peer (brother-in-law). In 1914 he joined up as an artillery officer and bid fair to become another Rupert Brooke, especially in his romantic love for England. But his lyricism began to peter out after 1917, partly because he considered himself primarily a dramatist. He taught in Tokyo and later was consultant to Douglas Fairbanks Sen. on films. He remained a picturesque high-minded figure, planning grandiose oeuvres *that somehow never reached completion.*

The Aftermath
VII SONNET: OUR DEAD

They have not gone from us. O no! they are
The inmost essence of each thing that is
Perfect for us; they flame in every star;
The trees are emerald with their presences.
They are not gone from us; they do not roam
The flow and turmoil of the lower deep,
But have now made the whole wide world their home,
And in its loveliness themselves they steep.

They fail not ever; theirs is the diurn
Splendour of sunny hill and forest grave;
In every rainbow's glittering drop they burn;
They dazzle in the massed clouds' architrave;
They chant on every wind, and they return
In the long roll of any deep blue wave.

WILFRED OWEN

(1893–1918)

Son of a Shropshire station-master, Owen assisted a vicar in a poor Oxfordshire parish, where his social indignation ousted his conventional Christianity. He taught English in France until, in 1915, he enlisted in the army and next year was sent to the Front. Already a minor, unpublished poet, he suddenly became a major one under the pressure of horror and compassion. During convalescence in hospital he had met Siegfried Sassoon who, sharing Owen's ironic reactions to 'glory', encouraged him to write. He returned to the Front in 1918 and, after winning the Military Cross, was killed one week before the Armistice.

Anthem for Doomed Youth

What passing-bells for these who die as cattle?
　Only the monstrous anger of the guns.
　Only the stuttering rifles' rapid rattle
Can patter out their hasty orisons.
No mockeries now for them; no prayers nor bells,
　Nor any voice of mourning save the choirs, –
The shrill, demented choirs of wailing shells;
　And bugles calling for them from sad shires.

What candles may be held to speed them all?
　Not in the hands of boys, but in their eyes
Shall shine the holy glimmers of good-byes.
　The pallor of girls' brows shall be their pall;
Their flowers the tenderness of patient minds,
And each slow dusk a drawing-down of blinds.

Futility

Move him into the sun –
Gently its touch awoke him once,
At home, whispering of fields unsown.
Always it woke him, even in France,
Until this morning and this snow.
If anything might rouse him now
The kind old sun will know.

Think how it wakes the seeds, –
Woke, once, the clays of a cold star.
Are limbs, so dear-achieved, are sides,
Full-nerved – still warm – too hard to stir?
Was it for this the clay grew tall?
– O what made fatuous sunbeams toil
To break earth's sleep at all?

from: Disabled

He sat in a wheeled chair, waiting for dark,
And shivered in his ghastly suit of grey,
Legless, sewn short at elbow. Through the park
Voices of boys rang saddening like a hymn,
Voices of play and pleasure after day,
Till gathering sleep had mothered them from him. . . .

One time he liked a blood-smear down his leg,
After the matches, carried shoulder-high.
It was after football, when he'd drunk a peg,
He thought he'd better join. – He wonders why.
Someone had said he'd look a god in kilts,
That's why; and maybe, too, to please his Meg;
Aye, that was it, to please the giddy jilts
He asked to join. He didn't have to beg;

Smiling they wrote his lie; aged nineteen years.
Germans he scarcely thought of; all their guilt,
And Austria's, did not move him. And no fears
Of Fear came yet. He thought of jewelled hilts
For daggers in plaid socks; of smart salutes;
And care of arms; and leave; and pay arrears;
Esprit de corps; and hints for young recruits.
And soon, he was drafted out with drums and cheers.

Some cheered him home, but not as crowds cheer Goal.
Only a solemn man who brought him fruits
Thanked him; and then inquired about his soul.

Now, he will spend a few sick years in institutes,
And do what things the rules consider wise,
And take whatever pity they may dole.
To-night he noticed how the women's eyes
Passed from him to the strong men that were whole.
How cold and late it is! Why don't they come
And put him into bed? Why don't they come?

HERBERT READ

(1893–1968)

Born and educated in Yorkshire, Read first experienced the adult world
in the trenches. After the war he became an original writer on art
and literature, a scholar, editor, biographer and critic. His theories on
aesthetics were developed while working in the Victoria and Albert
Museum and later in Edinburgh as Professor of Fine Art. He was
knighted in 1953. His war poems gained force and a cutting edge from
their use of clear images instead of romantic symbols (imagism). Some
are vividly horrible; all have a touch, however slight, of satire or
cynicism.

The Happy Warrior

His wild heart beats with painful sobs
his strain'd hands clench an ice-cold rifle
his aching jaws grip a hot parch'd tongue
his wide eyes search unconsciously.

He cannot shriek.

Bloody saliva
dribbles down his shapeless jacket.

I saw him stab
and stab again
a well-killed Boche.

This is the happy warrior,
this is he. . . .

from: *My Company*

I

You became
In many acts and quiet observances
A body and a soul entire.

I cannot tell
What time your life became mine:
Perhaps when one summer night
We halted on the roadside
In the starlight only,
And you sang your sad home-songs,
Dirges which I standing outside you
Coldly condemned.

Perhaps, one night, descending cold
When rum was mighty acceptable,
And my doling gave birth to sensual gratitude.

And then our fights: we've fought together
Compact, unanimous;
And I have felt the pride of leadership.

In many acts and quiet observances
You absorbed me:
Until one day I stood eminent
And I saw you gather'd round me,
Uplooking,
And about you a radiance that seemed to beat
With variant glow and to give
Grace to our unity.

But, God! I know that I'll stand
Someday in the loneliest wilderness,
Someday my heart will cry
For the soul that has been, but that now
Is scatter'd with the winds,
Deceased and devoid.

I know that I'll wander with a cry:
'O beautiful men, O men I loved,
O whither are you gone, my company?'

ISAAC ROSENBERG

(1890–1918)

Brought up in Whitechapel by working-class Jewish parents, Rosenberg was a gifted painter as well as poet. Educated in Stepney, he later trained at the Slade School of Art thanks to the generosity of three

Jewish women, and published his first extremely promising poetry at twenty-two. Two years later he visited a sister in South Africa to cure his 'weak lungs'. Returning home in 1915, he enlisted in the army despite his family's pacifism, and began his two years of trench warfare in 1916. He was killed on 1 April 1918. In one sense he was indeed a 'trench poet'. In another sense it is impossible not to feel that war was only accidentally the stimulus of a rich and varied genius.

from: TRENCH POEMS, 1916–1918

Break of Day in the Trenches

The darkness crumbles away –
It is the same old Druid Time as ever.
Only a live thing leaps my hand –
A queer sardonic rat –
As I pull the parapet's poppy
To stick behind my ear.
Droll rat, they would shoot you if they knew
Your cosmopolitan sympathies.
Now you have touched this English hand
You will do the same to a German –
Soon, no doubt, if it be your pleasure
To cross the sleeping green between.
It seems that you inwardly grin as you pass
Strong eyes, fine limbs, haughty athletes
Less chanced than you for life,
Bonds to the whims of murder,
Sprawled in the bowels of the earth,
The torn fields of France.
What do you see in our eyes
At the shrieking iron and flame
Hurled through still heavens?
What quaver – what heart aghast?
Poppies whose roots are in man's veins
Drop, and are ever dropping;
But mine in my ear is safe,
Just a little white with the dust.

The Jew

Moses, from whose loins I sprung,
Lit by a lamp in his blood
Ten immutable rules, a moon
For mutable lampless men.

The blonde, the bronze, the ruddy,
With the same heaving blood,
Keep tide to the moon of Moses.
Then why do they sneer at me?

Girl to Soldier on Leave

I love you – Titan lover,
My own storm-days' Titan.
Greater than the son of Zeus,
I know whom I would choose.

Titan – my splendid rebel –
The old Prometheus
Wanes like a ghost before your power –
His pangs were joys to yours.

Pallid days arid and wan
Tied your soul fast.
Babel-cities' smoky tops
Pressed upon your growth

Weary gyves. What were you
But a word in the brain's ways,
Or the sleep of Circe's swine?
One gyve holds you yet.

It held you hiddenly on the Somme
Tied from my heart at home.
O must it loosen now? I wish
You were bound with the old old gyves.

Love! you love me – your eyes
Have looked through death at mine.
You have tempted a grave too much.
I let you – I repine.

SIEGFRIED SASSOON

(1886–1967)

Born in Kent, Sassoon was one of the best known and, at first, least popular of the 'trench poets'. This was because of his intense revulsion from the war at a time when it was still idealised, and also because he survived it. He was thus able to continue writing, chiefly different forms of autobiography (the Sherston trilogy), a diary and religious poetry. He died a Roman Catholic. Three times he went to the Front and three times ended up in hospital. His contempt for 'them', the politicians and commanders who risked the lives of 'us', himself and his men, linked him to Owen and divided him from Brooke and Grenfell. He won the Military Cross for gallantry but threw it away.

Absolution
APRIL–SEPTEMBER 1915

This is how they felt when they first joined up. It was not to last.

The anguish of the earth absolves our eyes
Till beauty shines in all that we can see.
War is our scourge; yet war has made us wise,
And, fighting for our freedom, we are free.

Horror of wounds and anger at the foe,
And loss of things desired; all these must pass.
We are the happy legion, for we know
Time's but a golden wind that shakes the grass.

There was an hour when we were loth to part
From life we longed to share no less than others.
Now, having claimed this heritage of heart,
What need we more, my comrades and my brothers?

Blighters

4 FEBRUARY 1917

The tone has changed.

The House is crammed: tier beyond tier they grin
And cackle at the Show, while prancing ranks
Of harlots shrill the chorus, drunk with din;
'We're sure the Kaiser loves our dear old Tanks!'

I'd like to see a Tank come down the stalls,
Lurching to ragtime tunes, or 'Home, sweet Home',
And there'd be no more jokes in Music-halls
To mock the riddled corpses round Bapaume.

Base Details

ROUEN, 4 MARCH 1917

If I were fierce, and bald, and short of breath,
    I'd live with scarlet Majors at the Base,
And speed glum heroes up the line to death.
    You'd see me with my puffy petulant face,
Guzzling and gulping in the best hotel,
    Reading the Roll of Honour. 'Poor young chap,'
I'd say – 'I used to know his father well;
    Yes, we've lost heavily in this last scrap.'
And when the war is done and youth stone dead,
I'd toddle safely home and die – in bed.

Everyone Sang

APRIL 1919

The war is over.

Everyone suddenly burst out singing,
And I was filled with such delight
As prisoned birds must find in freedom,
Winging wildly across the white
Orchards and dark-green fields, on – on – and out of sight.

Everyone's voice was suddenly lifted;
And beauty came like the setting sun:
My heart was shaken with tears; and horror
Drifted away ... O, but Everyone
Was a bird; and the song was wordless; the singing will
    never be done.

CHARLES HAMILTON SORLEY

(1895–1915)

Sorley was the youngest to fall of these war poets – aged twenty. His England still meant the downs of his school, Marlborough. His collected poems, only thirty-seven in number, were entitled Marlborough and Other Poems, *with various subdivisions. His father was a professor at Aberdeen, where he was born, a Scot on both sides. His family moved to Cambridge in 1900. Having won a scholarship to Oxford, he was trapped on a summer walking-tour in Germany when war broke out. After one day in prison he was sent home, where he immediately applied for a commission. He died in the battle of Loos, leading his company in a successful attack on a 'hair-pin' trench.*

The Song of the Ungirt Runners

We swing ungirded hips,
And lightened are our eyes,
The rain is on our lips,
We do not run for prize.
We know not whom we trust
Nor whitherward we fare,
But we run because we must
   Through the great wide air.

The waters of the seas
Are troubled as by storm.
The tempest strips the trees
And does not leave them warm.
Does the tearing tempest pause?
Do the tree-tops ask it why?
So we run without a cause
   'Neath the big bare sky.

The rain is on our lips,
We do not run for prize.
But the storm the water whips
And the wave howls to the skies.
The winds arise and strike it
And scatter it like sand,
And we run because we like it
   Through the broad bright land.

from: *Of War and Death*

All the hills and vales along
Earth is bursting into song,
And the singers are the chaps
Who are going to die perhaps.
  O sing, marching men,
  Till the valleys ring again.
  Give your gladness to earth's keeping,
  So be glad when you are sleeping.

Cast away regret and rue,
Think what you are marching to.
Little live, great pass,
Jesus Christ and Barabbas
Were found the same day.
This died, that went his way.
  So sing with joyful breath,
  For why, you are going to death.
  Teeming earth will surely store
  All the gladness that you pour.

Earth that never doubts nor fears,
Earth that knows of death, not tears,
Earth that bore with joyful ease
Hemlock for Socrates,
Earth that blossomed and was glad
'Neath the cross that Christ had,
Shall rejoice and blossom too
When the bullet reaches you.
  Wherefore men marching
  On the road to death, sing!
  Pour your gladness on earth's head,
  So be merry, so be dead.

EDWARD THOMAS

(1878–1917)

Born in London, Thomas found that his private and withdrawn character was more suited to the countryside, though his early marriage made the problem of keeping his family by writing a constant anxiety. He met Robert Frost the American poet in 1913, and he persuaded Thomas to write poetry. All his poems were written from home, including those about the war. He seldom mentioned the war directly, as the 'trench poets' did, but it pervaded his verse nonetheless. He went out as an artillery officer and was killed by shell-blast at the battle of Arras. Fifty years later his reputation began to climb, and still stands high.

Thaw

Over the land freckled with snow half-thawed
The speculating rooks at their nests cawed
And saw from elm-tops, delicate as flower of grass,
What we below could not see, Winter pass.

Gallows 1916

This mock nursery rhyme, written near East Grinstead while Thomas was on leave, links the 'gallows' to the war, with almost hypnotic effect.

There was a weasel lived in the sun
With all his family,
Till a keeper shot him with his gun
And hung him up on a tree,
Where he swings in the wind and the rain,
In the sun and in the snow,
Without pleasure, without pain,
On the dead oak tree bough.

There was a crow who was no sleeper,
But a thief and a murderer
Till a very late hour; and this keeper
Made him one of the things that were,
To hang and flap in rain and wind,
In the sun and in the snow.
There are no more sins to be sinned
On the dead oak tree bough.

There was a magpie, too,
Had a long tongue and a long tail;
He could both talk and do –
But what did that avail?
He, too, flaps in the wind and rain
Alongside weasel and crow,
Without pleasure, without pain,
On the dead oak tree bough.

And many other beasts
And birds, skin, bone, and feather,
Have been taken from their feasts
And hung up there together,
To swing and have endless leisure
In the sun and in the snow,
Without pain, without pleasure,
On the dead oak tree bough.

The Trumpet

Written in training camp in England, autumn 1916.

Rise up, rise up,
And, as the trumpet blowing
Chases the dreams of men,
As the dawn glowing
The stars that left unlit

The land and water,
Rise up and scatter
The dew that covers
The print of last night's lovers –
Scatter it, scatter it!

While you are listening
To the clear horn,
Forget, men, everything
On this earth newborn,
Except that it is lovelier
Than any mysteries.
Open your eyes to the air
That has washed the eyes of the stars
Through all the dewy night:
Up with the light,
To the old wars;
Arise, arise!

POETS ELSEWHERE IN THE ABBEY

HENRY SPELMAN

(c. 1564–1641)

Historian, antiquary and ecclesiastical lawyer, Spelman was born in Congham, Norfolk, and lived either in Norfolk or London. He was an MP, a royalist and a devoted son of the Anglican Church. His scholarly writings included a history of Sacrilege, showing that no good came of using sacred buildings for lay purposes. (His son applied this doctrine to the Dissolution of the Monasteries, whereby Henry VIII had no grandchildren to succeed him and his family became 'extinct'.) Sir Henry Spelman is buried in the Abbey close to the entrance of St Nicholas's Chapel.

De Sepultura
ON BURIAL

Spelman denounced parsons who charged parishioners extortionate sums for burial, arguing that burial was natural and necessary.

As it is a Work of the Law of Nature and of Nations, of Human and Divine Law, to bury the Dead; so it is to administer that which necessarily conduceth to it, the *Place* and *Office of Burial*. If Man were so impious as not to afford it, the Earth to his shame will do it; she will open the Pores of her Body, and take in the

Blood; she will send forth her Children, the Worms, to bring in the Flesh of their Brother; and with her Mantle, the Grass, as with a Winding-sheet, she will enfold the Bones and bury all together in her own Bosom. Men (in passion) refuse oftentimes to do it to their Enemies, to wicked Persons, and to notorious Offenders; but she, as a natural Mother that can forget none of her Children, doth thus for them all, both good and bad; teaching us thereby what we should do for our Brethren, and branding those with Impiety that answer with *Cain, Am I my brother's Keeper?*

The Drift of my speech tendeth to the Reproof of a Custom grown up amongst *us Christians*, not heard of, I suppose, among the Barbarians; *Selling of Graves and the Duty of Burial.* . . .

Give me leave to present to you what I find in a Vestry-Constitution lately made, and subscribed by the Parson and Church-wardens, with three more of that Assembly, confirmed by the Bishop, approved by his Chancellor, declared to be a laudable Custom of that Parish, and in testimony thereof entered (as a solemn Act) in the principal Registry of the Lord Bishop of the Diocese; and finally ratified with the Chancellor's hand and seal of office: I may say, *vidi, puduitque videre* (I have seen, and have felt shamed to see).

Whosoever will be buried in the Church shall pay to the Parson as shall be agreed.

For interring the Corpse	10 shillings

IN THE ISLES OF THE CHANCEL

To the Church-wardens for the Ground	26 shillings 8 pence
To the Parson for interring the Corpse	6 shillings 8 pence

IN THE BODY OF THE CHURCH

To the Church-wardens for the Ground	20 shillings
To the Parson for interring the Corpse	6 shillings 8 pence

To the Parson for interring the Corpse
  coffined   2 shillings 8 pence
  uncoffined   1 shilling 4 pence

To him in like manner for every Child under seven Years. ...

Now it appeareth how this Grave-Silver or Money for Graves grew up to be taken; it was first given for praying for Souls and such like, but that being abolished and given to the King, the Parsons it seemeth take it for the Grave. And to say what I think, do now take that which was given for praying for the Soul, under their Fee for their Office of burying the Corpse, and this for the Grave besides, for they take both. But I say no more.

GEORGE HERBERT

(1593–1633)

Son of Sir Richard Herbert and brother of Lord Herbert of Cherbury (also a poet), George Herbert was born in Montgomery Castle and educated at Westminster and Trinity College, Cambridge. Despite an early yearning for the Church, Herbert became Public Orator at his university at twenty-five. A fine musician and singer, he was an orna-ment to James I's court. After James's death, he re-thought his life. Encouraged by his friends Nicholas Ferrar of Little Gidding and the poet John Donne, he decided on the Church, restoring the parsonage of Bemerton in Wiltshire, where he died of consumption three years later, leaving a young widow. His 'Metaphysical' poetry is still admired, link-ing as it did his sense of earthly beauty with God's intimate presence. A window on the south side of the nave is dedicated to Herbert and Cowper.

from: THE TEMPLE

Easter Wings

Herbert arranged his lines to resemble two pairs of wings.

Lord, who createdst the man in wealth and store,
Though foolishly he lost the same,
Decaying more and more,
Till he became
Most poor:

With Thee
O let me rise,
As larks, harmoniously,
And sing this day Thy victories:
Then shall the fall further the flight in me.

My tender age in sorrow did begin;
And still with sicknesses and shame
Thou didst so punish sin
That I became
Most thin.

With Thee
Let me combine,
And feel this day Thy victory;
For if I imp[1] my wing on Thine,
Affliction shall advance the flight in me.

[1] Engraft.

Virtue

Sweet day, so cool, so calm, so bright,
The bridal of the earth and sky,
The dew shall weep thy fall to-night;
         For thou must die.

Sweet rose, whose hue angry and brave
Bids the rash gazer wipe his eye,
Thy root is ever in its grave,
         And thou must die.

Sweet spring, full of sweet days and roses,
A box where sweets compacted lie,
My music shows ye have your closes,
         And all must die.

Only a sweet and virtuous soul,
Like season'd timber never gives;
But though the whole world turn to coal,
         Then chiefly lives.

The Pulley

When God at first made man,
Having a glass of blessings standing by,
'Let us', said He, 'pour on him all we can;
Let the world's riches, which dispersèd be,
    Contract into a span.'

So strength first made a way,
Then beauty flow'd, then wisdom, honour, pleasure;
When almost all was out, God made a stay,
Perceiving that, alone of all His treasure,
    Rest in the bottom lay.

'For if I should,' said He,
'Bestow this jewel also on My creature,
He would adore My gifts instead of Me,
And rest in Nature, not the God of Nature:
So both should losers be.

'Yet let him keep the rest,
But keep them with repining restlessness;
Let him be rich and weary, that at least,
If goodness lead him not, yet weariness
May toss him to My breast.'

from: SECULAR POEMS

Inscription in the Parsonage, Bemerton

TO MY SUCCESSOR

If thou dost find
An house built to thy mind,
   Without thy cost;
Serve thou the more
God and the poor;
   My labour is not lost.

ROBERT HOWARD

(1626–1698)

'*A Person of Quality*' *according to his own account, Howard was indeed distinguished by his parentage: his father was the Earl of Berkshire, his maternal grandfather the Lord Burghley. Howard fought gallantly for the King in the Civil War and was imprisoned in Windsor Castle by the victorious Parliamentarians. The Restoration brought him well-paid posts, though Mrs Uphill the actress is said to have consumed his fortune.*

The poet Dryden's brother-in-law, Howard wrote several plays with Dryden's help, and one lively comedy on his own. He is buried in the Chapel of St John the Baptist.

from: *The Committee*
ACT II

It is the 'Committee on Sequestration' – of Cavaliers' lands and possessions, under the chairmanship of Mr Day, a rapacious Roundhead. Mrs Arbella, the heroine, will have her estates sequestrated unless she marries Mr and Mrs Day's son Abel.

MR DAY   I pray withdraw; the Committee has passed their Order, and they must now be private.

COMMITTEE-MAN JOSEPH BLEMISH   [*To Mrs Arbella*] Nay, pray, Mistress, withdraw. [*Exeunt all but the Committee.*] So, Brethren, we have finished this day's work; and let us always keep the bonds of unity unbroken, walking hand in hand, and scattering the Enemy.

MR DAY   You may perceive they have spirits never to be reconciled; they walk according to Nature, and are full of inward darkness.

BLEMISH   It is well truly for the good people, that they are so obstinate, whereby their estates may of right fall into the hands of the Chosen, which truly is a mercy.

MR DAY   I think there remaineth nothing further, but to adjourn till Monday. Take up the papers there, and bring home to me their Honours' order for Mrs Arbella's estate. So, Brethren, we separate ourselves to our particular endeavours, till we join in public on Monday, two of the clock; and so peace remain with you. [*Exeunt.*]

from: *A Song for Two Cavalier Colonels*
ACT IV SCENE ONE

They are the two heroes, Colonel Blunt and Colonel Careless.

Now the veil is pulled off, and this pitiful Nation
Too late see the Gull of a Kirk-Reformation,
    How all things that should be
    Are turned topsy turvy;
    The freedom we have,
    Our Prince made a slave,
And the Masters must now turn to Waiters.
    The great ones obey,
    While the rascals do sway,
And the loyal to rebels are traitors.

JOHN BUNYAN

(1628–1688)

Born in Elstow near Bedford, John was descended from generations of Bunyans, Binyans or Buniuns in the same village. His father, a tinker or brasier, sent him to the village school. John himself became an 'inspired tinker'. As a parliamentary boy-soldier in the first Civil War, he learnt to swear, but his 'godly' young wife cured him. After much spiritual anguish he was born again as a popular Nonconformist preacher, though already criticised by Episcopalians for trying to mend souls as well as kettles. He was arrested after the Restoration for breaking the renewed laws against unlicensed preaching. Imprisoned for 12 years, God visited him, as he saw it, with the idea of Pilgrim's Progress – *that tremendous allegory of human life. After his release, the authorities ignored his preaching. In the west aisle of the north transept a window is dedicated to him.*

from: *The Pilgrim's Progress*

Mr Valiant-for-truth is approaching the climax of his pilgrimage.

'Who would true valour see,
　Let him come hither;
One here will constant be,
　Come wind, come weather;
There's no discouragement
Shall make him once relent
His first avowed intent
　　　　　To be a pilgrim.

Whoso beset him round
　With dismal stories,
Do but themselves confound;
　His strength the more is.
No lion can him fright,
He'll with a giant fight,
But he will have a right
　　　　　To be a pilgrim.

Hobgoblin nor foul fiend
　Can daunt his spirit;
He knows he at the end
　Shall life inherit.
Then fancies fly away,
He'll fear not what men say;
He'll labour night and day
　　　　　To be a pilgrim.'

THE PASSING OF MR VALIANT-FOR-TRUTH

After this it was noised abroad that Mr Valiant-for-truth was
taken with a summons by the same post [messenger] as the other
[Mr Honest], and had for a token that the summons was true,

that his pitcher was broken at the fountain. (Ecclesiastes, xii 6.) When he understood it, he called for his friends, and told them of it. Then said he, 'I am going to my Father's; and, though with great difficulty I have got hither, yet now I do not repent me of all the troubles I have been at to arrive where I am. My sword I give to him that shall succeed me in my pilgrimage, and my courage and skill to him that can get it. My marks and scars I carry with me, to be a witness for me that I have fought His battles who will now be my rewarder.' When the day that he must go hence was come, many accompanied him to the river side, into which as he went he said, 'Death, where is thy sting?' And as he went down deeper, he said, 'Grave, where is thy victory?' (I Corinthians, xv 55.) So he passed over, and all the trumpets sounded for him on the other side.

WILLIAM CONGREVE

(1670–1729)

Prince of Restoration comedy, Congreve was born in Yorkshire but educated at Trinity College, Dublin, owing to his father's employment in Ireland. As one of the many writers who turned from the law to literature, he won esteem, financial rewards, valuable government posts, important friends such as Alexander Pope, and the love of the Duchess of Marlborough, who bore him a natural daughter. His most famous play, The Way of the World, *showed the world as a riot of intrigue, deceit and folly, though there was still a place in it for the loving and faithful. His bust is in the south aisle.*

from: *The Way of the World*
ACT IV SCENE ONE

The lovers Millamant, 'a fine lady', and Mirabell, are setting their conditions for marriage.

MIL My dear liberty, shall I leave thee? my faithful solitude, my darling contemplation, must I bid you then adieu? ... my morning thoughts, agreeable wakings, indolent slumbers, all ye *douceurs*, ye *sommeils du matin*, adieu? – I can't do't, 'tis more than impossible – positively, Mirabell, I'll lie abed in a morning as long as I please.

MIR Then I'll get up in a morning as early as I please.

MIL Ah! idle creature, get up when you will – and d'ye hear, I won't be called names after I'm married; positively I won't be called names ... as wife, spouse, my dear, joy, jewel, love, sweetheart, and the rest of that nauseous cant, in which men and their wives are so fulsomely familiar – I shall never bear that – good Mirabell, don't let us be familiar or fond, nor kiss before folks ... nor go to Hyde Park together the first Sunday in a new chariot, to provoke eyes and whispers, and then never to be seen there together again; as if we were proud of one another the first week, and ashamed of one another ever after. Let us never visit together, nor go to the play together; but let us be very strange and well-bred; let us be as strange as if we had been married a great while; and as well-bred as if we were not married at all.

MIR Have you any more conditions to offer? Hitherto your demands are pretty reasonable.

Millamant goes on to assert her right to receive any visits or letters;

MIL ... to have no obligation upon me to converse with wits that I don't like, because they are your acquaintance: or to be intimate with fools, because they may be your relations. ... to be sole empress of my tea-table. ... And lastly, wherever I am, you shall always knock at the door before you come in. These articles subscribed, if I continue to endure you a little longer, I may by degrees dwindle into a wife.

MIR Your bill of fare is something advanced in this latter account. – Well, have I liberty to offer conditions – that when you are dwindled into a wife, I may not be beyond measure enlarged into a husband?

MIL You have free leave; propose your utmost, speak and spare not.

Mirabell insists that she have no secret female confidante nor go to the play in a mask;

MIR ... that you continue to like your own face as long as I shall: and while it passes current with me, that you endeavour not to new-coin it. To which end, together with all vizards for the day, I prohibit all masks for the night, made of oiled-skins, and I know not what – hogs' bones, hares' gall, pig-water, and the marrow of a roasted cat. ... *Item*, when you shall be breeding –

MIL Ah! name it not.

MIR Which may be presumed with a blessing on our endeavours.

MIL Odious endeavours!

MIR I denounce against all strait lacing, squeezing for a shape, till you mould my boy's head like a sugar-loaf, and instead of a man child, make me a father to a crooked billet. Lastly, to the dominion of the tea-table I submit – but with proviso, that you exceed not in your province; but restrain yourself to native and simple tea-table drinks, as tea, chocolate, and coffee: as likewise to genuine and authorised tea-table talk – such as mending of fashions, spoiling reputations, railing at absent friends, and so forth – but that on no account you encroach upon the men's prerogative, or presume to drink healths, or toast fellows. ...

All strong waters to be banished, though cowslip and poppy wine are allowed.

MIR These provisos admitted, in other things I may prove a tractable and complying husband.

MIL O horrid provisos! Filthy strong-waters! I toast fellows! odious men! I hate your odious provisos.

MIR Then we are agreed! shall I kiss your hand upon the contract?

WILLIAM COWPER

(1731–1800)

Cowper's profound piety, his home and garden, his friends and pets saved him from becoming the extreme depressive that always threatened. Son of a country clergyman, he early developed melancholia that is thought to have been exacerbated by at least five factors: a sickly disposition, his mother's early death, bullying at his private school, sense of sin, failure to get a job or get married. He made two suicide attempts. Nonetheless, his poems and letters showed a tranquil domesticity that could float free from his psychological entanglements. Though himself a 'Stricken Deer', his perceptive view of the natural world set him apart from the usual artificialities of the eighteenth century. He is commemorated with George Herbert in a window on the south side of the nave.

Epitaph on Fop

A dog belonging to Lady Throckmorton.

Though once a puppy, and though Fop by name,
Here moulders one, whose bones some honour claim;
No sycophant, although of Spaniel race!
And though no hound, a martyr to the chase.
Ye squirrels, rabbits, leverets, rejoice!
Your haunts no longer echo to his voice.
The record of his fate exulting view.
He died worn out with vain pursuit of you.

'Yes!' the indignant shade of Fop replies,
'And worn with vain pursuit man also dies!'

from: *Light Shining out of Darkness*

God moves in a mysterious way
　　His wonders to perform;
He plants his footsteps in the sea,
　　And rides upon the storm.

Ye fearful saints, fresh courage take,
　　The clouds ye so much dread
Are big with mercy, and shall break
　　In blessings on your head. . . .

Blind unbelief is sure to err,
　　And scan his work in vain:
God is his own interpreter,
　　And he will make it plain.

from: *The Task*
BOOK III: THE GARDEN

On Puss, his pet hare. In a note Cowper wrote that Puss, his hare, died aged 11 years 11 months. Puss would come to divert him when he was mentally and physically sick. When later Cowper nursed the sick hare, she expressed gratitude 'by licking my hand, first the back of it, then the palm, then every finger separately, then between all the fingers, as if anxious to leave no part of it unsaluted.'

　　One shelter'd hare
Has never heard the sanguinary yell
Of cruel man, exulting in her woes.
Innocent partner of my peaceful home,
Whom ten long years' experience of my care
Has made at last familiar; she has lost
Much of her vigilant instructive dread,
Not needful here, beneath a roof like mine.
Yes, – thou mayst eat thy bread, and lick the hand
That feeds thee; thou mayst frolic on the floor

At evening, and at night retire secure
To thy straw couch, and slumber, unalarm'd;
For I have gained thy confidence, have pledged
All that is human in me to protect
Thine unsuspecting gratitude and love.
If I survive thee, I will dig thy grave;
And, when I place thee in it, sighing say
I knew at least one hare that had a friend.

EDWARD BULWER-LYTTON

(1803–1873)

Son of General Bulwer and a Lytton heiress, Edward Bulwer-Lytton became a Reform MP at twenty-eight, possessing a dramatic sense of social and political change. This inspired him to write five novels romanticising change in different eras: The Last Days of Pompeii, Rienzi, the last of the Roman Tribunes, The Last of the Barons, Harold, the last of the Saxons, *and* The Coming Race *(science fiction). A fashionable dandy, he scrapped with Tennyson and pleased Disraeli. His son became Viceroy of India, his granddaughter a leading Suffragette. He was given a peerage and the memorial to the 1st Lord Lytton is in the Chapel of St Edmund.*

from: *The Last Days of Pompeii*

The witch-like hag of Vesuvius, after a visit from Arbaces, the villainous Egyptian, gets a terrifying preview of the catastrophe to come.

She replaced the stone [concealing her treasure], and continued her path onward for some paces, when she stopped before a deep irregular fissure in the earth. Here, as she bent – strange, rumbling, hoarse, and distant sounds might be heard, while ever and anon, with a loud and grating noise which, to use a homely but faithful simile, seemed to resemble the grinding of steel upon wheels, volumes of streaming and dark smoke issued forth, and rushed spirally along the cavern.

'The Shades are noisier than their wont,' said the hag, shaking her grey locks; and, looking into the cavity, she beheld, far down, glimpses of a long streak of light, intensely but darkly red. 'Strange!' she said, shrinking back; 'it is only within the last two days that dull deep light hath been visible – what can it portend?'

Lytton's picture of the break-up of a civilisation in the eruption.

Wild – haggard – ghastly with supernatural fears, these groups [of fugitives] encountered each other, but without the leisure to speak, to consult, to advise; for the showers [of cinders and rock] fell now frequently, though not continuously, extinguishing the lights, which showed to each band the death-like faces of the other, and hurrying all to seek refuge beneath the nearest shelter. The whole elements of civilisation were broken up. . . . you saw the thief hastening by the most solemn authorities of the law, laden with, and fearfully chuckling over, the produce of his sudden gains. If, in the darkness, wife was separated from husband, or parent from child, vain was the hope of reunion. Each hurried blindly and confusedly on. Nothing in all the various and complicated machinery of social life was left save the primal law of self-preservation!

In the fearful confusion, Glaucus and Ione, the betrothed Greek couple, meet their deadly foe, Arbaces the Egyptian; Glaucus threatens to destroy him if he lays a finger on Ione.

Suddenly, as he spoke, the place became lighted with an intense and lurid glow. Bright and gigantic through the darkness, which closed around it like the walls of hell, the mountain shone – a pile of fire! Its summit seemed riven in two; or rather, above its surface there seemed to rise two monster shapes, each confronting each, as Demons contending for a World. These were of one deep blood-red hue of fire, which lighted up the whole atmosphere far and wide; but, below, the nether part of the mountain was still dark and shrouded, save in three places, adown which flowed, serpentine and irregular, rivers of the molten lava. ... And through the stilled air was heard the rattling of the fragments of rock, hurtling one upon another as they were borne down the fiery cataracts – darkening, for one instant, the spot where they fell, and suffused the next, in the burnished hues of the flood along which they floated!

Arbaces, standing in front of a towering bronze statue of Augustus Caesar, believes the eruption to be favourable to his designs.

He advanced one step – it was his last on earth! The ground shook beneath him with a convulsion that cast all around upon its surface. A simultaneous crash resounded through the city, as down toppled many a roof and pillar! – and lightning, as if caught by the metal, lingered an instant on the Imperial Statue – then shivered bronze and column! Down fell the ruin, echoing along the street, and riving the solid pavement where it crashed! – The prophecy of the stars was fulfilled!

The sound – the shock, stunned the Athenian for several moments. When he recovered, ... his eyes were fixed upon a ghastly face that seemed to emerge, without limbs or trunk, from the huge fragments of the shattered column – a face of unutterable pain, agony, and despair! The eyes shut and opened rapidly, as if sense were not yet fled; the lips quivered and grinned – then sudden stillness and darkness fell over the features, yet retaining that aspect of horror never to be forgotten!

So perished the wise Magician – the great Arbaces – the Hermes of the Burning Belt – the last of the royalty of Egypt.

The statue representing Imperial Rome and the man representing ancient Egypt had crashed together. Glaucus and Ione were to escape to Athens and convert to Christianity; there had been Christians in Pompeii – the religion of the future.

CHARLES KINGSLEY

(1819–1875)

Born in Devon, Kingsley followed his father into the Church, rising to be a canon of Westminster and Professor of Modern History at Cambridge. He was known as a 'muscular Christian' whose aggressive Protestantism in the end was counter-productive, for in trying to nail Roman Catholic 'lies' he provoked Cardinal Newman into writing his world-famous Apologia. *Kingsley's great strength lay in genuine and articulate sympathy with the victims of social injustice (unless they were black) and a brilliant visual imagination that appealed to all classes and ages. Like Lewis Carroll, he is remembered most affectionately for two children's books:* The Heroes *and* The Water-Babies. *He is commemorated by a bust in St George's Chapel.*

When All the World is Young

G. K. Chesterton, though himself an ardent Roman Catholic, described this poem as the best argument ever produced in favour of marriage.

> When all the world is young, lad,
>   And all the trees are green;
> And every goose a swan, lad,
>   And every lass a queen;
> Then hey for boot and horse, lad,
>   And round the world away;
> Young blood must have its course, lad,
>   And every dog its day.
>
> When all the world is old, lad,
>   And all the trees are brown;
> And all the sport is stale, lad,
>   And all the wheels run down;

Creep home and take your place there,
The spent and maimed among:
God grant you find one face there,
You loved when all was young.

JAMES RUSSELL LOWELL

(1819–1891)

Another son of the clergy and a poet of distinction in many spheres, Lowell was born in Cambridge, Massachusetts, and educated at Harvard. He is one of those who found his inspiration in poetry after first trying the law. He succeeded Longfellow as Professor of Modern Languages at Harvard, while Longfellow was later to succeed him as editor of the North American Review; *Lowell having already founded and edited the prestigious* Atlantic Monthly. *He entered the diplomatic service at fifty-eight and lived in London for five years as American Minister. He had already written for the Liberal* Daily News. *His high-mindedness and humour made his poetry as popular as his company was welcome. His memorial is in the vestibule of the Chapter House.*

from: *Stanzas on Freedom*

Inspired by the great Slavery conflict.

Men! whose boast it is that ye
Come of fathers brave and free,
If there breathe on earth a slave,
Are ye truly free and brave?
If ye do not feel the chain,
When it works a brother's pain,
Are ye not base slaves indeed
Slaves unworthy to be freed?

from: *The Present Crisis – December 1844*

Once to every man and nation comes the moment to decide,
In the strife of Truth with Falsehood, for the good or evil
  side;
Some great cause, God's new Messiah, offering each the
  bloom or blight,
Parts the goats upon the left hand, and the sheep upon the
  right,
And the choice goes by forever 'twixt that darkness and that
  light.

from: *At the Commencement Dinner, 1866*
IN ACKNOWLEDGING A TOAST TO THE SMITH PROFESSOR

I rise, Mr Chairman, as both of us know,
With the impromptu I promised you three weeks ago,
Dragged up to my doom by your might and my mane,
To do what I vowed I'd do never again;
And I feel like a good honest dough when possesst
By a stirring, impertinent devil of yeast.
'You must rise,' says the leaven. 'I can't,' says the dough;
'Just examine my bumps, and you'll see it's no go.'
'But you must,' the tormentor insists, 'tis all right;
You must rise when I bid you, and, what's more, be light.' . . .
  'Tis a dreadful oppression, this making men speak
What they're sure to be sorry for all the next week. . . .
  They say it is wholesome to rise with the sun,
And I daresay it may be if not overdone;
(I think it was Thomson[1] who made the remark
'Twas an excellent thing in its way – for a lark;)
But to rise after dinner and look down the meeting
On a distant (as Gray[2] calls it) prospect of Eating –

---

[1] James Thomson, *The Seasons*.
[2] Thomas Gray, *A Distant Prospect of Eton*.

Professor Lowell finds the prospect appalling – but after another forty lines he capitulates and finds his solution.

Now since I've succeeded – I pray do not frown –
To Ticknor's and Longfellow's classical gown,
And profess four strange languages, which, luckless elf,
I speak like a native (of Cambridge) myself,
Let me beg, Mr President, leave to propose
A sentiment treading on nobody's toes, . . .
A toast that to deluge with water is good
For in Scripture they come in just after the flood:
I give you the men but for whom, as I guess, sir,
Modern Languages ne'er could have had a professor,
The builders of Babel, to whose zeal the lungs
Of the children of men owe confusion of tongues;
And a name all-embracing I couple therewith,
Which is that of my founder – the late Mr Smith.

NOËL COWARD

(1899–1973)

Son of a Middlesex piano salesman, Coward was dedicated to the theatre as actor, playwright and composer of songs and musicals. He lived to see many of his popular comedies revived. He had an ear for dialogue in his light comedies and his songs had memorable lines. His floor-stone is in the south choir aisle.

from: WORDS AND MUSIC

Mad Dogs and Englishmen

Mad dogs and Englishmen
Go out in the midday sun.
The Japanese don't care to,
The Chinese wouldn't dare to,

Hindoos and Argentines sleep firmly from twelve to one,
But Englishmen detest a
Siesta.

In the Philippines there are bamboo screens
To protect you from the glare.
In the Malay States there are hats like plates
Which the Britishers won't wear.

At twelve noon the natives swoon
And no further work is done.
But mad dogs and Englishmen
Go out in the midday sun.

from: THIS YEAR OF GRACE

Dance Little Lady

Though you're only seventeen,
Far too much of life you've seen,
Syncopated child.
Maybe if you only knew
Where your path is leading to
You'd become less wild.
But I know it's vain,
Trying to explain
While there's this insane
Music in your brain.

Dance, dance, dance, little lady!
Youth is fleeting to the rhythm beating
In your mind.
Dance, dance, dance, little lady,
So obsessed with second best,
No rest – you ever find.
Time and tide and trouble
Never, never wait,
Let the cauldron bubble,
Justify your fate.
Dance, dance, dance, little lady!
    Leave to-morrow behind.

Poor Little Rich Girl

Poor little rich girl,
You're a bewitched girl,
Better beware
Laughing at danger,
Virtue a stranger,
Better take care!
The life you lead sets all your nerves a-jangle,
Your love affairs are in a hopeless tangle,
Though you're a child, dear,
Your life's a wild typhoon,
In lives of leisure,
The craze for pleasure,
Steadily grows.
Cocktails and laughter
But what comes after?
Nobody knows.
You're weaving love into a mad jazz pattern,
Ruled by pantaloon.
Poor little rich girl, don't drop a stitch too soon.

The Stately Homes of England

The Stately Homes of England
How beautiful they stand,
To prove the upper classes
Have still the upper hand;
Though the fact that they have to be rebuilt
And frequently mortgaged to the hilt
Is inclined to take the gilt
Off the gingerbread.

Index